THE BUDDHA WALKS INTO THE OFFICE

ALSO BY LODRO RINZLER

The Buddha Walks into a Bar . . .

Walk Like a Buddha

THE BUDDHA WALKS INTO THE OFFICE

A Guide to Livelihood for a New Generation

Lodro Rinzler

Shambhala / Boston & London / 2014

Shambhala Publications, Inc.
Horticultural Hall
300 Massachusetts Avenue
Boston, Massachusetts 02115
www.shambhala.com

9 8 7 6 5 4 3 2 1

First Edition
Printed in the United States of America

⊗This edition is printed on acid-free paper that meets the
American National Standards Institute Z39.48 Standard.
♻This book is printed on 30% postconsumer recycled paper.
For more information please visit www.shambhala.com.

Distributed in the United States by Penguin Random House LLC
and in Canada by Random House of Canada Ltd

Library of Congress Cataloging-in-Publication Data
Rinzler, Lodro.

The Buddha walks into the office: a guide to livelihood
for a new generation / Lodro Rinzler.—First edition.
    pages   cm
Includes bibliographical references and index.
ISBN 978-1-61180-061-6 (alk. paper)
1. Business—Religious aspects—Buddhism.
2. Interpersonal relations—Religious aspects—Buddhism.
3. Quality of work life. 4. Spiritual life—Buddhism.
I. Title.
BQ4570.B86R56 2014
294.3'444—dc23
2013043415

In memory of my father, Carl Rinzler

CONTENTS

PREFACE

Sometimes at work people are jerks. Sometimes you are one of them. This book is about how not to be a jerk (which, in retrospect, might have been a better title) and how to work with others in your office so that mindfulness and empathy can flourish.

After my first book, *The Buddha Walks into a Bar*, came out, I found myself being viewed as the Buddhist author equivalent of George W. Bush. I myself was not fond of that gentleman's politics but remember clearly that when he was running for president, people seemed magnetized to him for a very specific reason: they could see themselves having a beer with that man.

For whatever reason, I think that's what happened to me. I didn't intend to write with a casual tone, but let's face it: I'm not the most senior, learned teacher at your local monastery. I'm a guy who has sat on his butt meditating for more hours than he'll admit, has given some thought to how that meditation practice affects his life, and is good at drinking beer. So when people reached out to me after reading my first book, often they would invite me to have a drink with them the next time I was in town.

The thing is, more often than not, when you go out and get a beer with someone, you end up talking about work. If I get a beer with younger friends, we talk about what it means to be a young person finding your way, developing a livelihood that you feel good about. If I get a beer with friends who are not as young, we talk about how hard it is to apply meditation principles to our nine to five.

I realized that after the bar, there's the morning commute. Because in my travels people wanted so much to talk about applying Buddhism to the workplace, this seemed like a natural thing to discuss.

So this book is both a continuation of my first books and actually much more focused. I'm not going to rehash every aspect of Buddhist philosophy from *The Buddha Walks into a Bar* or discuss as many topics as *Walk Like a Buddha*. Instead, we're going to dive into the nitty-gritty work of work. How can you bring mindfulness, the act of being present, and compassion off the meditation cushion and into this place we spend most of our waking hours? Specifically, for those of you familiar with the various turnings of the wheel of dharma, or the Buddha's teachings, this is a book that deals with Mahayana teachings, that is, teachings on bringing an open mind and heart to all of our worldly interactions. This is a guidebook to becoming the kind of authentic leader this world needs.

I have been a meditation practitioner and instructor longer than I have been in the workforce, and thus the philosophy of Buddhism has permeated my own workplace interactions. Ultimately, that led me to found the Institute for Compassionate Leadership, a six-month training program that partners the philosophy offered in this book with other methodologies aimed at creating a new generation of openhearted and genuine individuals. The wisdom in this book is the small amount that I have been able to retain in my years of study with my Buddhist teachers and professional mentors. The rest of it is based in the fact that if there is a mistake to be made on the Buddhist path—or the path of office life—I have likely made it and, often, learned from it.

All of this said, you let me know how it strikes you. Because, as was the case with the other books, the most important part is the conversation that comes after you read this book. I wrote it for you, and I continue to be here for you, so please reach out. We'll get a beer and talk about work.

Lodro Rinzler

ACKNOWLEDGMENTS

Thank you for taking the time to read this book; I hope you connect with it in some way.

Shambhala Publications has been a tremendous support for this book. I would like to thank Sara Bercholz for providing encouragement and space to work from, even though she insisted on taking photographic documentation of me passing out at my computer on a semiregular basis. My editor, Dave O'Neal, has been such a joy to work with over these past few years. I am fascinated by his mind and his quick wit. I am lucky to have him. Jonathan Green has been my number-one fan and has been so patient with me as an author. Daniel Urban-Brown has designed the covers for my books, and I owe him a debt of gratitude. In fact, I am indebted to everyone at Shambhala.

I would like to acknowledge Susan Piver and Michael Carroll for their incredible care and mentorship throughout the process of this book/my professional life. Stephanie Tade is the best agent one could ask for in this business.

So many of my friends have been wonderful in encouraging my work as an author. With that in mind I would like to thank David Delcourt, Brett Eggleston, Oliver Tassinari, Ethan Nichtern, Will Conkling, Miranda Stone, Christine Espinoza, Josh Silberstein, Maron Greenleaf, David Perrin, Jeff Grow, Eric French, Matt Bonaccorso, Dilip Sidhu, Annie Colbert, Victoria Gerstman, and Noah Isaacs. Similarly, I would like to thank my parents, Beth and Carl Rinzler, as well as my brother, Michael, and my sister, Jane.

There are a number of other individual close to me, whose love and stories have shaped this piece. With that in mind I would like to thank Laura Sinkman, Tom Krieglstein, Marina Klimasiewfski, Liz McKenna, Erin Peavey, Liza Kindred, Ericka Phillips, Arshad Chowdhury, Sean Gavin, Lucy McKenna, and Hylke Faber.

Oddly enough, much of this book, unlike *The Buddha Walks into a Bar*, was written in a bar. I would like to thank the entire staff at Sophie's in the East Village of New York for providing me with such lovely office space.

None of my writing would be possible without the influence of Sakyong Mipham Rinpoche, whom I am honored to call my teacher. I am fortunate to have all of you in my life.

PART ONE

HINAYANA

Live with Purpose

1 / SETTING AN INTENTION

Most of us spend a sizable chunk of our waking hours at work. Many of us don't even enjoy the work we are engaged in day after day, or see it as a means to bankroll our free time. I'm a firm believer that with the right view—one based in becoming more awake to your everyday life, one that is grounded in knowing why you do what you do—you can live a happier, fuller life in and out of the workplace. You can live a life based around qualities you want to cultivate in yourself and qualities you want to see flourish in the world.

After my first book came out, I traveled quite a bit for it. I would do events at meditation centers, bookstores, and universities. Early on in the book tour, I gave a talk at Yale. I met two young women there, both on the verge of graduating. The first woman (I'll call her Jess) took me on a campus tour and led me to a Starbucks for coffee. Making conversation, I casually asked her, "What do you think you want to do after graduation?" I'm always careful to ask what people want to do, or where they might want to live, as opposed to that nerve-racking "What are you going to be when you grow up?" question.

"It's funny you ask that here," Jess said, "because I want to become the chief marketing officer for Starbucks." She went on to describe how much her happiness related to attaining that goal. I thought this was an interesting choice. Out of all the industries in the world, she had picked one already. Not only that, but she had picked one specific company in that industry, and she aspired to one specific role within that company. I don't remember being that sure of my career path when I was in my early twenties—or of anything else, for that matter. Furthermore, I know several people who would never consider such a lofty ambition possible, based on how they were raised. Still, I wished Jess luck and chatted a bit with her to see why she was interested in that path.

Later that evening, I met another young woman and asked her the same question. I'll call her Christine. "Me?" she asked. "I have no idea what I want to do. And it terrifies me." This struck me as a genuine answer, one that felt closer to my own experience ten years prior: I had no idea what I wanted to do but was open to exploring my options, as groundless as that experience may be. As I continued to travel on the book tour, I began to see this was a common sentiment among young people on the verge of entering the "real world." Very few of them had it all figured out, which is a scary state, yet full of possibility.

I don't think Christine is in a better or worse position than Jess. In my opinion, there is nothing wrong with wanting to succeed in life. If you aspire to make a positive impact in the world, that is lovely. Also, you can aspire to have material comforts, like a home and clothes; there's nothing in the Buddhist canon that says you shouldn't have them, just that you should not be attached to them.

However, if we base all our happiness on attaining something as specific as one position in one company, we may end up disappointed. Jess, who wants to be the CMO of Starbucks, could find herself spending decades on that goal and miss out on other aspects of her life in pursuit of it. She could end up turning a blind eye to other interesting career choices, or turning down romantic pursuits to focus on her CMO goal, or missing opportunities for fun and connection with others. And, at the end of the day, if she does not attain that position as the CMO of Starbucks, then she will be unhappy.

Here's the funny thing: If Jess does attain her goal, she could still be unhappy! She could end up disliking aspects of it, such as working long hours, or feeling she is underpaid or underappreciated. Alternatively, she might just find that position isn't what she thought it was and hatch a plan to move to a new position or company. With such a fixed idea of what she wants to be when she grows up, she could, I feared, be in for a lifetime of dissatisfaction.

Christine, in contrast, was terrified about what she was going to do for a career, but she said she is trying to remain open to whatever might enter her life. Without the same sense of direction as our future CMO, she seemed more likely to explore her world without buying into the belief that she has to have it all figured out.

As I continued to travel and talk with different people, this theme of livelihood came up over and over. I am (perhaps) annoyingly curious, so I found myself talking with people from all different walks of life, whether they were travel companions, attending a book event, or just sitting next to me at a bar. I spoke with doctors, tattoo artists, grad students, waiters, entrepreneurs, and exotic dancers. The interesting thing all of these people had in common is that they didn't let their job define who they are. The idea they had stumbled onto is that in searching for happiness, it was not so much a question of what they did as why they did it.

Knowing your intention is key in all things. If you want to meditate, it's important to know why you want to meditate. It is a difficult and gradual path, and as such it can be disheartening at times, so when you find yourself shying away from your meditation cushion, it's helpful to have a strong reason you chose to pursue such a practice.

Similarly, it is important to know why we do what we do in other aspects of our life. Why are you going out to drink with friends? Is it because you haven't seen them in a long time and want to connect over a glass of wine? Or is it because you can't deal with the frustrations of your job at the restaurant and need to blow off steam? When it comes to figuring out a career path, knowing your intention may be the most basic and most helpful step on the journey that links your work with your spiritual path.

THE THREE YANAS

This book is organized around the three *yanas*, a Sanskrit word that can be translated as "vehicle." From a Tibetan Buddhist point of view, there are three yanas that we can apply to our life in order to truly explore the paths of mindfulness and compassion. These three vehicles are the means to transport us from our confusion to awakening. They each serve specific purposes and emphasize different aspects of the Buddhist canon. At the same time, all are important, interpenetrate, and once learned can and should be practiced at once.

In the first section, we explore the *Hinayana* path, which allows us to dive into the work of discovering what right livelihood means in today's world and, more important, to each of us individually. Right livelihood is one of the eight aspects of living a good and thoughtful life that the Buddha articulated more than 2,500 years ago. It is the idea that we have to include certain activities in how we work so that we are being of benefit to ourselves and others. Even centuries after the Buddha, the notion of doing a job that is "right" because we are being thoughtful about our work is still incredibly relevant today.

While I represent a lineage that uses the term *Hinayana*, I am not fond of it, as it has been used as a derogatory term in some texts; it is often translated as "narrow vehicle." It is the path of learning to be authentic to yourself, through developing an in-depth understanding of who you truly are. This is a process of self-discovery, where you are keeping a narrow focus on learning about both your neurosis and your wisdom. As I come from a Tibetan Buddhist perspective, I acknowledge that

Hinayana is something of a loaded term; I don't mean any offense. In fact, the Hinayana path is based in working with your own mind and heart in order to build a foundation to apply mindfulness and compassion in every aspect of your life. In that sense, it's not narrow at all!

From there, in the next two sections we explore the second vehicle, the Mahayana path, and focus on offering our hearts in the area where we spend most of our waking hours: our job. The Mahayana journey is one of extending yourself well beyond your comfort zone and approaching your life and work from the perspective of what is good for everyone, not just yourself. It is opening your heart to the world and letting that open heart create true change in society. We will explore tools on compassion and leadership that we can all engage in to bring the Buddhist principles of being present and empathetic into every aspect of our work. Along with the aspiration to be of benefit to everyone we encounter, there are also specific skillful means offered, such as the six *paramitas* and Six Ways of Ruling.

When we are proficient at this, we are prepared for the third vehicle, the Vajrayana, which is based in the view that our work and our role in society are all part of our spiritual journey. On this path, we no longer view the world in terms of what is for us versus what is against us; every joy and disappointment in our work becomes fodder for our path of awakening. We treat our workplace as a sacred environment, in which whatever occurs is a lesson we can learn and a way to improve ourselves as genuine people.

The steady hand guiding us in these three vehicles is meditation. The Tibetan word for meditation is *gom*, which can be more literally translated as "become familiar with." Through the practice of meditation, we are becoming familiar with ourselves, our aspirations, and our intentions. The more we are familiar with why we want to do any given thing, the more confidence and care we put into it.

The Power of Listening
to Your Intention

My first job out of college was to serve as the executive director of a meditation center in Boston, a thirty-five-year-old nonprofit with a lot of history, in both the positive and the negative sense. It was a pretty big deal that the board of directors had trusted me—a twenty-two-year-old with no business experience whatsoever and a complete unknown in that organization—with the keys to that particular castle. Even before moving to Boston, I heard rumors of people voicing their concern and asking the board to reconsider hiring someone so young.

The day I arrived, there was an annual celebration for that Buddhist community. I was introduced to the members of the center and was invited to say a few words after I officially took on my position. I had prepared a speech, but when I got up in front of the hundred-plus members that day, I could only speak from my heart. "My intention," I said, "is to be genuine and fearless. I may run this place into the ground, but I will do so genuinely and fearlessly."

With no business background, I held on to that intention for dear life. In the first year, I worked with the community to institute a new generosity policy for all of our classes; we were bursting at the seams with new members; and the organization, which had traditionally run at a deficit of $10,000 to $20,000, was in the black for the first time in years. I had taken some big risks, but I did so in line with my initial intention, and as a result things seemed to have worked out.

In contrast to that, I remember a time when I had a clear intention but didn't stick to it. Several years ago, I decided that I wanted to move away from nonprofit work and try my hand at something more lucrative. I longed to be of benefit to society but wanted simultaneously to try to achieve more worldly success. I found a position as the head of operations for a consulting company, and initially I thought it would be a good fit. It was a business devoted to nurturing other small businesses, trying to support the mom-and-pop organizations of the world. I thought working there would be in line with both my intention to make good money and my intention to help others—a win-win.

Over time, though, I stuck with the good-money intention and watched as the other one drifted off into the sunset. If I had paid more attention to my environment, then I probably wouldn't have ignored so many of the signs that this company was not the right one for me. But I had put my blinders on.

As I continued to learn more about the company, I found the signs harder to ignore. The CEO was constantly behind on payroll for her small but devoted staff, yet she lived in a giant apartment in the West Village of New York City (from which we had to work when she couldn't pay our office rent). The company couldn't hold on to an employee for more than a year because of the high expectations and mistreatment of the staff. The small businesses that we were supposed to be helping were few and far between, and the CEO spent all her time schmoozing investors.

Within a few months, I was the most senior employee, and despite the paycheck I could no longer convince myself that what I was doing was of benefit to anyone (including myself). I quit that job amicably and went back to doing work that felt like it was in line with my intention to help others.

These two experiences taught me a lot about what I need to be happy. The bottom line is that my intention, while constantly changing as I grow older, seems to be about trying to be of benefit to society. If I become familiar with that intention in its current manifestation, then I find myself successful and happy. If I stray from it in an attempt to base my happiness solely in material gain like money or special benefits, then I may find some temporary satisfaction but end up exhausted and discontent in the long term.

This idea of internal exploration is the beginning of the Buddhist path. Before we go into the office and work with others in a way that is of benefit, we first have to know ourselves well.

Once we know ourselves well, we can be true to who we are. The first step is to know our intention—both large intentions, like knowing why we are engaging in our line of work, and smaller ones, such as knowing what we want to accomplish on a given day. This is the foundation of our path. This is the heart of the journey. Knowing our own intention, the why behind the what, is an important first step.

CONTEMPLATION FOR SETTING YOUR INTENTION

When you first wake up in the morning, it might be helpful to reflect on your intention for that day. This is not the massive "What am I going to make of myself?" question. It can be much simpler. You could say, *I aspire to be a bit kinder than yesterday* or *My intention is to be a bit more patient when I get frustrated with my coworkers.* Take a moment to reflect on what it is you want to make of your day, even before you get out of bed.

Alternatively, you could sit down and meditate before engaging in this contemplation. In the next chapter, we will get into formal meditation instruction, which is the basis for this work of becoming familiar with ourselves. It is helpful to engage in this practice as a way to feel grounded. Your daily intention may come up at the end of your meditation session, or you might need a minute or two afterward to come up with it.

Then, enter your day. If it is helpful, you could even write down your intention someplace where you will see it. It could be a sticky note on your desk or a Word document on your laptop. This can help remind you to come back to your intention over and over again, just as you come back to the breath during formal meditation practice.

At the end of your day, sit down and reflect on how you did in manifesting your intention. This is not where you get judgmental and down on yourself; quite the opposite. It is a great time to offer yourself gentleness and a sense of friendliness.

If you want to get to know someone, you don't begin by judging them on everything they do wrong. You start by approaching them with a sense of inquisitiveness and openness. You are gentle in the getting-to-know-you process. The same goes for becoming familiar with yourself. With that in mind, take a moment each night and gently ask yourself how you did in following through on your intention.

Were there a few times that day when you were kind to others? Did you keep your cool when your coworker would not shut up in that meeting? If so, you can rejoice in that. If not, then tomorrow is another day to practice this contemplation. If you completely forgot about your intention today, that's okay. If you remember your intention only twice the next day, that's a marked improvement! The more we are familiar with ourselves and our intention, the more we can find happiness in all aspects of our life, especially our work. From that point onward, you can, with all your heart, give yourself to it.

2 / DISCOVERING OUR WORTHINESS: AN INTRODUCTION TO MEDITATION PRACTICE

Zazen practice and everyday activity are one thing.

—*Shunryu Suzuki Roshi*

It is foolish for us to think that we can separate our work life and our meditation practice. Wherever we are, we have the ability to be present. On the meditation cushion, we can be present with the physical sensation of our breathing. Off the cushion, we can be present with the people we encounter, the experience of our morning commute, the food we eat, everything. That is the purpose of meditation practice: to become more present and aware of every aspect of our life.

When it comes to work, we always have a choice. We can schlep through our day-to-day existence, considering those hours we are working a waste of time, constantly looking ahead to our time off, or we can engage it in a way that makes us feel like we are participating in a life worth living. Meditation practice helps us slow down and be present enough to recognize the small joys about our work as well as its frustrations. It helps us sort through the muck of our own mind, know our intention clearly, and live our lives fully.

One Tibetan word for meditation (there are several) is *samten*. If you break it down further, *sam* is "mind" and *ten* is "strong." In other words, meditation practice is the way to develop a stable and flexible mind. A strong and flexible mind is an obvious asset both in determining what you want to do with your life and for performing well in your chosen livelihood. With the proper view, you do not have to differentiate developing this strong mind on the meditation cushion from your work experience. They can be one and the same.

The Buddha practiced meditation under a number of teachers, and each time he would achieve an amazing, magical, transcendent experience. He would go back to these teachers and say, "So, is that it? That's what you do?" These teachers would be impressed that he had mastered their meditation so quickly and say, "Yes, that's it! That's the experience. Don't you feel holy now?" The Buddha, I imagine, wouldn't be so impolite as to say, "Hell, no," but he did walk away from these instructors.

After some time, he sat down under a tree and just did a simple meditation on his breath. It grounded him in the reality of the present moment, what is going on right now. Through that experience he achieved what is often referred to as enlightenment. What was he enlightened to? The reality of the way things are. He became able to see how things work in the world, the truths of how we suffer and create confusion for ourselves and others, and how he could stop doing that.

This meditation practice that he did, and that we can do, is not about achieving those magical, other-worldly states that he was introduced to early on in his path. It's about being present to the way things are. This is known as *shamatha*, or calm-abiding meditation. The more we can connect with the present in a calm way in our life and our work, the more we can be of use to the world around us. The more present we are, the less stressed-out we will be, and the more we can perform admirably, with a strong mind as our support.

INSTRUCTIONS FOR MEDITATION PRACTICE

The most important thing to do before you begin practicing meditation is to relax. This might sound silly—isn't that what meditation is supposed to do for us? Unfortunately, more often than not, people take their meditation practice too seriously, feeling like they have to "get it right." They get uptight about practicing meditation, which means they are undoing the very thing they are trying to achieve.

My root teacher, Sakyong Mipham Rinpoche, has emphasized this idea of relaxing before you try to meditate. If you sit down in a rushed manner and try to cram in ten minutes of meditation before you jump off the cushion and accomplish a thousand things, your mind will not slow down in the least.

So it may be helpful to ease into meditation. This might mean taking a minute to drink a glass of water or a mug of tea, or stretching, or reading a bit from a Buddhist book, or just taking a few deep breaths before you sit down. The idea is to not go into your meditation practice with your mind at sixty miles per hour but ideally to relax to the point where maybe your mind is running at twenty or thirty miles per hour. Taking the time to enter your meditation practice properly pays off.

ENVIRONMENT

Sometimes people ask me if you need to buy a meditation cushion to meditate at home. I don't think so, at least not as you begin your practice, but it can be helpful. Simply having a meditation cushion in your home reminds you that you have the option of meditating. Every time you see it, you think, "Oh, right, I really ought to do that today." If you don't want to invest, though, take a cushion from your couch or a pillow from your bed and sit down on it.

Another way to create an environment for your meditation practice is to set up a small but permanent area with a candle, a bowl with incense in it, or a statue of the Buddha. These simple reminders really do make a world of difference in carving out an area of your home where you are inspired to practice meditation consistently. It is important to set aside a place, if only a corner of your living room, where you consistently go to meditate. There are enough other obstacles to meditation; re-creating your practice space each day shouldn't have to be one of them.

You want to sit in an area of your home where you feel a sense of spaciousness. This means not sitting in front of your television or computer, not sitting a foot from a wall, and generally staking out some relatively quiet territory where you get some light. When you sit down there, you want to feel like you are being supported by the environment, not that it is infringing on your state of mind.

POSTURE

Once you have staked out where you will meditate and you feel like you have created some mental space so you can meditate properly, sit on a cushion or chair and connect with your body. There are six main points to remember when taking a good meditation posture:

1. *Seat.* You should feel grounded when you sit down to meditate. That means sitting in the center of your cushion or chair, not feeling like you are about to fall forward or tensing up and leaning back. Sit like a king or queen upon their throne. You should feel that kind of dignity and upliftedness when you sit down to meditate.

2. *Legs.* If you are sitting on a cushion, your legs can be loosely crossed with your knees falling a little lower than your hips. If you are in a chair, sit with your feet firmly on the floor.

3. *Torso.* Having established this strong base, you can extend upward, connecting with a sense of spaciousness around you. You can imagine that your spine is a stack of quarters, one on top of the other, all the way up to

your skull. Connecting with that image of a strong skeletal structure, you can relax the muscles in your shoulders and back. You don't have to force your body to be upright. You can rely on your spine's natural curvature. If you find yourself slouching over (and we've all been there), take a moment to reconnect with your strong base and bring yourself back up, leading with your head.

4. *Hands.* Various traditions of meditation encourage you to do different things with your hands. My recommendation is to pick your arms up, bending at the elbows, and drop your palms down on your thighs. That should be a comfortable spot for your hands and will also provide a bit more support for your back.

5. *Eyes.* In the spirit of relaxing into the present moment, relax your eyes. You can keep them open, resting your gaze somewhere two to four feet ahead of you on the ground. Don't fixate on what you are staring at; relax your gaze. We keep our eyes open as a reminder that we are trying to wake up to our present experience.

6. *Mouth.* Further relaxing the muscles in your face, including around your forehead, cheeks, and jaw, you might find that your mouth hangs open. That is encouraged. Keeping the mouth slightly open allows air to move more easily through your mouth and nose. The tip of your tongue can rest on the roof of your mouth.

The overall point of this posture is to keep you upright, feeling a sense of dignity, and yet relaxed. You don't have to overthink these six points, but they are good ones to check in on when you sit down to meditate.

BREATH

Meditation is not about forcing yourself to do or achieve anything; it's about relaxing into the present moment. Because you don't have to do anything, you can be gentle and nonjudgmental with yourself. Take a moment at this point to remind yourself to be gentle during your meditation period.

Having grounded yourself in your body, turn your attention to your breath. Follow the physical sensation of both your in-breath and your out-breath. You breathe all the time, so this is just being present with what you are already doing. You don't need to alter your breathing in any way; just bring your mind to it. This is what is known as mindfulness, the simple act of bringing yourself fully, one-pointedly, to what you are doing.

This is not the most exciting practice in the world, but the fact that it is basic means that you are not going to be prone to too many distractions. The breath is simple. It is always fresh. It is what is going on in this instant. As such, you can stay fully present with your breath and just let thoughts come and go as if they were clouds passing across the sky.

COME BACK, OVER AND OVER AGAIN

The tricky part is that thoughts will come up. Sometimes they will look discursive—you'll start thinking about all the things you need to accomplish later in the day. Sometimes they will look like full-blown fantasies—you'll start having an argument with someone who isn't even in the room. Sometimes you may feel struck by a strong emotion like passion or anger, and various story lines will start spinning out around that emotional upheaval. In all these situations, the instruction remains the same: come back to the breath. Come back to what is going on right now.

If it is helpful, you can silently say *thinking* to yourself when a thought takes root in your mind. This is not a moment to become aggressive and yell at yourself: *THINKING!* Instead, take a very gentle approach to your mind. As mentioned in the previous chapter, if you want to become familiar with yourself, you need to treat yourself well. So be kind to yourself, and very gently remind yourself that you seem to be wandering off from the present moment, which is not what you intended to do.

Acknowledging that, you say *thinking* and come back to the breath.

That is the basic meditation practice. It's what the Buddha did, and if it's good enough for him, it should be good enough for us. We don't need to try to change it or improve upon it. Its simplicity is part of its magic. There are times when we love it and times when we can't wait to leap off our meditation seat. This is natural. In fact, if you sat down in a room full of meditators and asked them to raise their hands if they have ever thought that they were the worst meditator in the history of meditation, a vast majority of people would raise their hands.

Practicing meditation is like a roller coaster. Sometimes we feel "up" and are resting with the breath continuously. Then we sit down the next day, and we feel like we might as well throw our hands up in the air and scream as we ride down, down into the depths of discursiveness. We all do this.

However, if we can train in coming back to the breath, over and over again, what we are really doing is training in being present with this very moment. When we get off the meditation cushion, our life is filled with millions of this very moment. As we train ourselves, we can be present with those and live our lives with just as much mindfulness as we developed on the meditation cushion.

As the meditation teacher and author Pema Chödrön has said, "We don't sit in meditation to become good meditators. We sit in meditation so that we'll be more awake in our lives."

BASIC GOODNESS

Pema Chödrön highlights the idea that we don't practice meditation to become a "good meditator." I have given the word *good* a great deal of thought. So often people are trying to be a "good" something: A good employee. A good husband. A good mother. A good meditator. When we consider this notion, good is very relative. We compare ourselves to others and use them as markers for how good we are. We are a better employee than

Ethan, who always comes in late, but not as good as Annie, who seems to volunteer to spearhead all kinds of after-hours projects. That is often how we determine if we are a "good" employee. (If you want a great read on being a "good mother," get Tina Fey's *Bossypants*, though she's much funnier than I am, and I haven't given birth to anyone yet.)

I am a practitioner and teacher in the Shambhala Buddhist tradition, which has its roots in Tibetan Buddhism but encourages meditation as a tool that anyone from any religious background can use to wake up more fully to their world. In the Shambhala tradition, the term *good* has a particular connotation. We use the term *basic goodness* frequently in Shambhala. This notion is a 180-degree turn from the Catholic notion of original sin. It's the view that we are not inherently bad at all; underneath our layers of confusion, pain, and aggression, we're actually basically good.

The idea of basic goodness is that at your core you are innately wise. You are innately kind. You are innately capable. That's your birthright. That is who you are. When we talk about the Buddha attaining enlightenment, it is said he realized his Buddha nature, the seed within each of us that is naturally awake, naturally aware. Buddha nature is the ability that each of us has to follow in the Buddha's footsteps and achieve our own awakening.

Basic goodness, our very nature, is what we are waking up to. It is the notion that at the core of everything, we have this unwavering source of strength and power—our innate goodness.

Here is the good news: if we are innately wise and kind and good, then we are also innately worthy. Two years ago I gave a talk in New Haven, and a gentleman named Michael raised his hand at the end. Meditation is all fine and good, he said, but at the end of the day he felt that he was not as well trained or educated as his colleagues. "I feel a lack of confidence at work—that I'm not smart enough or capable enough to succeed there."

I don't think Michael is alone. Many of us raised in a materialistic society have had advertising and consumer culture inform us that we are too dumb or too fat or too young (or old) to be what we want to be. The notion of basic goodness is that we all are capable, if we can bring ourselves to act from the point of view of our basic goodness. We have everything we need and can offer ourselves as we are. As one wise friend once told me, "You're worth what you think you're worth." So you should probably start recognizing that you are worth a great deal.

Basic goodness is that stillness we experience after a meditation session. It is that sense of calm that we tap into when we are not caught up in the storm of our swirling emotional upheavals and wild fantasies. It is always available to us, if we are able to become present enough to see it.

As the author Wayne Dyer has said, "Change the way you look at things, and the things you look at change."[1] The practice of meditation can make seemingly insurmountable obstacles appear like minor hurdles. If we can learn to be present, to touch our basic goodness and act from it, then we can accomplish anything.

Tips for Practicing Meditation at Work

I recommend that people start their day with meditation, when their mind is fresh. However, the best time for meditating will look different for different people. Some people love to meditate when they get home from work. Others like to take some time in the middle of the day, during their lunch break. Regardless of what works for you, try to start off with ten minutes a day, as many days a week as you can. It is said that after eleven consecutive days of doing anything, it starts to become a habit, so if you want to start meditating regularly, try sticking to it for that period. And, to kick a dead horse, be gentle with yourself. Over time, if you miss a day here or there, no need to beat yourself up. Relax.

That daily meditation practice can be the foundation of your spiritual journey. However, it would be foolish to think that you leave your mindfulness on the meditation cushion when you're done with a session. We are, after all, practicing for something. That something is the rest of our life.

Since we spend so much time at work, it is helpful to take moments to practice meditation throughout our day. My friend Adam Lobel is a great meditation teacher. Adam was blessed with a child while in his twenties, and as any parent knows, it's hard to make your own schedule when you have a little one. The fascinating thing I found with Adam is that whenever he had space in his day, he would turn it into a short meditation session. He accomplished what Shunryu Suzuki Roshi spoke about: blending everyday activity with meditation practice.

I think any of us can follow Adam's lead. If we have one meditation session at some point in our day, we can use that as the jumping-off point for very short sessions throughout the rest of it.

With that in mind, there are a few techniques I recommend for practicing meditation at your workplace, be it a post office, an auto-body shop, a library, or even a busy department store.

THE DING MEDITATION

One thing I like to do is set a timer to go off once an hour. I set a reminder on my phone, and after sixty minutes it goes *ding!* No matter what I am working on, I am reminded to raise my gaze, connect with my posture, and meditate for a minute. I don't set a timer for the meditation itself; I just practice for what feels like a minute or two, then reset the timer and go back to work.

THE RED DOT MEDITATION

My very first meditation instructor offered me this technique when I expressed interest in meditation as a child. He knew I would grow restless if I had to sit still for long periods, so he recommended I take red circular sticker dots (you can find them at any stationery store) and post them around my house. When I walked by one and noticed it, I would think of it as a tiny STOP sign and pause, connect with my body, pay attention to my breath for a few moments, then move on. Try this in your own work environment. These little dots are small enough that very few people will notice them, and seeing them cuts through the habitual way you might rush about the place.

THE BUDDY SYSTEM

It's often helpful to have a community of other meditators who encourage you to practice regularly. Is there someone else in your place of employment who is interested in meditation? If so, you two can carve out some time during lunch or another break and meditate together for ten minutes. Find a quiet spot on the grass outside or on a bench somewhere, set a timer, and enjoy each other's support. Granted, it is extraordinary to find this sort of spiritual friend at work, but if you can, you will experience a great level of support for your meditation practice. It's worth asking your colleagues if they are interested.

The more we begin to offer ourselves the gift of meditation, both in longer sessions and in little moments throughout our day, the more we can experience the present moment and enjoy it as an opportunity to connect with our basic goodness. From there, our strong mind can support us throughout our day.

3 / BE WHO YOU WANT TO BE

Find something you love to do and you'll never have to work a day in your life.

—*Harvey Mackay*

When I was seven years old, my first-grade teacher asked everyone to draw what they wanted to be when they grew up. I remember walking around my classroom during parent-teacher night with the walls plastered with drawings, learning all about my classmates' long-term aspirations. Who knew? It was a room full of aspiring astronauts and baseball players.

I have to admit, I was the odd man out. My picture portrayed a man hunched over a typewriter, working away at his book. Even recalling that image today makes me sit up straight at the keyboard.

As all of us grew up, though, we found ourselves part of an interesting generation. Although often referred to as Generation Y (because we came along after Generation X, who were born between 1960 and 1980), my generation, due to our supposed apathy, has earned a new nickname: Generation Why. Apparently we did not follow in the footsteps of previous generations, set on overthrowing systems and causing a revolution. We had video games and the Internet, and that kept us to ourselves.

Then along came a fantastic presidential campaign in 2008. Regardless of what political party you may feel an affinity for, you have to admit that "Change we can believe in" has a sweet sound to it. We Generation Yers came out in droves to vote, and for our dedication we earned a new nickname: Generation O (as in Obama). Many of us felt that finally Change with a capital C was possible.

ECONOMIC DEPRESSION AND LACK OF DIRECTION

At the same time, change has not come quickly, and our economic situation has led to widespread disheartenment. Some members of my generation were raised with parents and teachers telling them they could be whatever they wanted to be when they grew up. Yet, when twenty-somethings enter the workforce today, they quickly realize that this simply is not true.

My former classmates who grew up aspiring to sports stardom or wishing to travel the stars may now be settling for unpaid internships. Maybe those internships aren't even in the field they wanted to pursue originally.

We now face a time when there simply isn't room in this economy for the notion that if you work hard enough, you can do anything you want to do. With the scarcity of opportunities in the job market, more and more young people are becoming discouraged and looking for any work they can find.

An older friend of mine who works as a therapist told me that many of the twenty-somethings she meets with feel they have been told that the economy has improved and opportunities are once again available. That means that if these individuals can't find a job, it's not the fault of society; it's their lack of capability. Such a message is disheartening.

On top of that level of discouragement and lack of opportunity is the fact that many of us still haven't figured out what we want to be when we grow up. (I don't think this term *grow up* applies just to twenty-somethings, mind you. Many of my friends who are in their sixties still don't think of themselves as grown up.) Many of us in Generation O have been told that we ought to know what we are doing with our lives by age twenty-two, or twenty-five at the latest. And many of my peers simply still have no idea.

This is reflected in the expression *quarter-life crisis*. I remember mine: I felt ready to leave my job as the executive director of a meditation center, yet the funding for my next job in development had not come through. I remember sitting at my desk one night at midnight, filling out half a business school application, then realizing that I had to take a standardized test but couldn't do the test and submit the application within the forty-eight hours left before the deadline, and applying for a dozen executive assistant jobs in New York City. Incidentally, these jobs pay $80,000 to $100,000 a year but are apparently miserable. I was freaking out.

The next day I woke up and practiced meditation and, thankfully, relaxed. I realized I didn't need to have everything sorted out. I practiced patience; the funding for my development job came through; and only years later do I feel like I am doing exactly what I want to be doing. In fact, if I hadn't gone through this process, I likely wouldn't have been able to found the Institute for Compassionate Leadership, whose six-month program trains people in meditation and empathy development so that they can move from the general idea of wanting to help the world to a finding their specific purpose and empowering them to do that work (for more information, see the resources section).

MAPPING OUT WHO YOU WANT TO BE WHEN YOU GROW UP

A few years ago, at dinner with my friend Laura, I was talking about my writing and she about her impending graduation from social work school. Both of us felt on the cusp of something career-like, but we had to pause and acknowledge that this year was the first time in our adult lives we had really revisited that old idea of "what do you want to be when you grow up." We started mapping out the trajectories for all of our mutual friends. They too had hit their late twenties and were suddenly scrambling to figure out what they wanted to do with the rest of their lives.

It occurred to me that given the current educational and economic situation in the United States, maybe the question of what you want to be when you grow up is outdated. This conversation steered me toward what is perhaps a better question for the thoughtful young person today: "*Who* do you want to be when you grow up?"

I found that in determining *who* you want to be when you grow up, it is helpful to physically map some things out for yourself. And a mandala can be useful as a map. One transla-

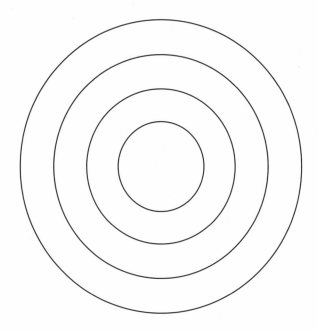

tion of the Sanskrit word *mandala* is "circle." It is a diagram often used in Buddhism to depict the abode of a deity or a microcosm of the universe. A mandala can be viewed in some respect as a sort of organizational chart, with a circle at its center and several concentric circles around it. In the traditional mandala representing what is known as the Wheel of Life, at the center there are representations of three poisonous emotions that keep us stuck in suffering—passion, aggression, and ignorance. We will explore these three facets of our mind in chapter 5. In the next concentric circle there is a symbolic representation of karma. The third circle illustrates the six realms of existence. Both karma and the six realms will be covered in depth in chapter 10. The outermost circle depicts how we create a solid sense of self, or ego (chapter 21), and other illustrations represent impermanence and how we can escape this cycle by following the example of the Buddha. The Wheel of Life shows us how we continuously create a world of suffering by holding at our core three habitual reactions to the world—passion, aggression and ignorance. The idea in the Wheel of Life mandala and the one depicted here is that what is at the center of the mandala influences everything else in it. We can think of our lives and livelihood in those terms. Here is a fun exercise I encourage you to engage in:

1. Copy the diagram above by drawing a circle, then drawing three to five circles around it, in a concentric manner.
2. Meditate for ten minutes.
3. Toward the end of that meditation session, ask yourself, "What qualities do I want to cultivate in myself?"
4. Write down those qualities on a separate piece of paper. Be concise—just a few words will do. It might be *kindness, sincerity, wisdom,* or something equally personal to you.
5. Look at those qualities. Let your mind rest on them. As you rest your mind, discern which feel most pertinent.
6. If there is one that really stands out, write that down at the center of your mandala. For some people it might

read *feeling less stressed-out all the time* or *being more gentle* or *practicing compassion.* Try to make it a quality rather than a job title.

7. In the circle outside of that center, write down some people or things that are important to you. You might write the names of family members or your partner, or hobbies you engage in, or (I recommend this one) what you do or aspire to do for a living. Continue in the next circle out with other aspects of your life. Do you run? Put that in there. Do you like museums? Singing? Put those down. Continue to fill out the circles you drew with various aspects of your life. The more important they are to you, the closer they belong to that innermost circle.

8. Draw a line from the core of the mandala to each of those things you have written down.

9. On each of those lines, write how you might want your core motivation to influence that aspect of your life. For example, if you wrote down *kindness,* what would shift in that connection to your boss? What would shift in how you spend your money? What would shift in how you exercised?

10. When you are done writing, place the paper aside and rest with whatever feelings have come up. Then return to formal shamatha meditation, staying with your breath for five minutes.

RIGHT LIVELIHOOD

An exercise like this one can help you determine what qualities you want to cultivate in your life. When the Buddha began teaching, he laid out what is known as the Noble Eightfold Path. This path is made up of eight elements that he encouraged his disciples to follow in order to find freedom from suffering and in so doing to develop wisdom, ethical conduct, and meditative discipline. One of the three elements of ethical conduct in this path (along with right speech and right action) is right livelihood—that is, making your living in a way that doesn't create harm.

Traditionally, right livelihood refers to being employed in a legal and peaceful way. However, opinions about what "peaceful" might mean have varied dramatically over the 2,500-plus years since the Buddha taught. It is generally agreed that there are five specific aspects to right livelihood:

1. You can't deal in living beings; this includes activities like prostitution, slavery, or raising animals for slaughter.
2. You can't make money selling weapons.
3. You can't make money selling poison.
4. You can't make money selling intoxicants.
5. You can't make money selling meat.

Even these five aspects of right livelihood can be interpreted in a number of ways. If we strictly interpret this list, it would prohibit working as an exterminator, bartender, or butcher or even in a deli selling sandwiches because you would be profiting from selling meat.

However, to pull back from the traditional teachings on this topic, the bottom line seems to be that right livelihood means that we do not cause harm to others or ourselves. If you hold that idea in your heart as you engage in your contemplations on career, then you will likely end up causing less suffering to others and enjoying what you do.

You Are Not Your Job

When you engage in an exercise like the ten steps earlier, you are switching your focus from questions about what you ought to be doing with your career and instead embracing an idea of who you want to be. This will be helpful as you engage your career path, because you can always cultivate the qualities that are important to you, whereas you may not always be able to make a living doing exactly what you want to do.

Furthermore, if you define your identity as your job, you will end up discontent. Sometimes people think that they *are* their specific job, and if they are fired or promoted, they have a bit of a crisis: "I was the pivotal person who held that department together, but now I'm not there and they are still operational. What happened?"

The bottom line is that you are not your job. I remember attending a leadership conference in Halifax, Nova Scotia, and walking into the bathroom, only to receive a profound teaching on this topic. Written on the bathroom stall were the words, "This is your life and it is ending second by second." Sure, I thought, life is impermanent.

Then I noticed that right below that scrawl were these words: "This is not your life. This is a bathroom stall. If you think this is your life you should be concerned." Brilliant! In the same way, your job is not your life. If you think your life is your job, you should be concerned. Your life is what you make of it and what qualities you want to cultivate during your time here on earth.

Now, imagine for a moment a world where an entire generation took the view that it is more important that they determine who, not what, they want to be when they grow up. Some would still become baseball players and astronauts, but they would engage their work with the values that are most important to them.

If my generation and future generations took up this simple question, we would not squander years trying to find the "perfect" job. We would discern what is important to us and live all aspects of our life in line with what we actually wanted to be. I am a firm believer that by doing that we would ultimately create that Change in society with a capital C.

THE BUS STOP MEDITATION

Tom is a serial entrepreneur. I've known him for a while and am often impressed by the thoughtfulness he puts into making decisions. The other year he left a company he cofounded and struck out on his own. I asked him about his process for figuring out his next step, and he offered me what he called a "bus stop meditation."

Imagine yourself sitting on a bench, keeping an open mind. As you sit there, buses will pull up. Each bus represents a potential opportunity. It could be a high-paying job in a new field, or an idea for a new start-up, or just a chance to try something new at the risk of a lower-than-average salary. Some of these buses might look appealing, and you can check them out, but you have to refrain from immediately jumping on one.

The practice here is simply to notice the bus. You watch the idea instead of leaping on it out of panic or desire. You investigate it. You can ask yourself, "If I got on that bus, where would I end up in five or ten years? What would my life look like?"

As you watch the buses go on their way, there will be some that really strike you as interesting and others that you are glad you didn't hop on. Because it's a bus route, more often than not similar buses will come back around.

Before you hop on any bus, though, you can take the time to really research it. You can talk to friends and mentors about the idea, or even just poke around the Internet, and consider whether this is the right bus for you.

Tom could have done any number of things. Instead of freaking out and jumping on the first appealing bus that came his way, he was able to just be present to whatever arose. Eventually, he narrowed down his options to three, did his research, and then climbed aboard. Today he is the founder of a successful company that allows university alumni and major corporations to direct their donations to specific causes that current students are passionate about.

When I asked him why he chose that bus over all the others that came his way, he told me about his root motivation. "I was a Boy Scout," he said. "We have a motto: Always leave the campsite better than you found it." With that motivation at the core of who he is, Tom could have jumped on any of these buses and left the world a better place. His ability to discern the right bus for him is a direct result of his ability to be present.

4 / WIELDING YOUR SPEECH
LIKE THE HAMMER OF THOR

Work is also something real, just as much as spiritual practice. So work doesn't have to have any extra meaning behind it, but it is spirituality in itself.

—Chögyam Trungpa Rinpoche, *Work, Sex, Money*

There is a common misunderstanding that if you are going to be a "good" Buddhist, you will have to leave your career and run off to the woods to meditate 24/7 until you reach enlightenment. I don't think you have to do that in order to follow a spiritual path.

I have seen my Buddhist teachers engage students on the topic of livelihood over and over again. Often it comes up at the end of a talk, when people are invited to ask questions. Every time someone gets up to speak about their job, they probably think they are unique in feeling overwhelmed by their level of responsibility and what is expected of them, or in feeling underappreciated for what they do. They could be executives at marketing firms or work long hours at a busy chain restaurant. The question remains the same: "How," they ask, "can I possibly live a spiritual life and engage this line of work?"

I think we all feel, at one point or another, that we have to take our spirituality (that thing we do on a meditation cushion for twenty minutes in the morning) and place it in one realm, and take our livelihood (that other thing we do for eight to twelve hours a day) and hold them apart, so never the two shall meet.

As Chögyam Trungpa Rinpoche points out, we don't have to suffer from this self-inflicted dichotomy. If you can shift your view so that your work is spirituality, then you can bring your meditation practice off the cushion and live your hours at work with meaning and purpose.

Thus far we have looked at two ways of engaging our work as part of our spiritual journey. The first is contacting our own innate abilities, our basic goodness, through the practice of meditation. The second is becoming inquisitive with ourselves, so that we can determine who we want to be as we live our lives and engage our livelihoods in a way we feel good about.

If you can ground yourself in these two activities, you can show up at work and be successful while staying true to yourself. You could be toiling away as an intern at Goldman Sachs, trying to start your own nonprofit, working as a truck driver, stocking shelves at a Walmart, or serving in the armed forces. No matter what you do, if you bring into your work basic goodness and the qualities you want to cultivate and let those be your guiding principles, then you will have great success.

Unfortunately, most of our colleagues are not following this simple principle. They try to engage their work from the point of view of their own afflictive emotions, as opposed to their own goodness. As my teacher, Sakyong Mipham Rinpoche, has said, "We're often confused about our purpose in the world, because we mistakenly associate worldly activity with negative emotion. We think that being successful means accomplishing what we want with ambition and greed. Being trapped by negative emotions and perpetuating them is not worldly success—it is worldly ignorance."[1]

I am guessing that the last thing you want to do is perpetuate worldly ignorance. Yet, when we are careless with our speech, we often end up causing harm and adding fuel to the fire of negative emotions. If you want to avoid causing harm, you must learn to wield your speech as a weapon for good.

USING YOUR SPEECH AS A WEAPON OF DELIGHT

In Norse mythology, Thor is the god of thunder. In traditional texts and, more recently, in comic books, he wields a mighty war hammer known as Mjölnir. This weapon has incredible power and possesses the strength to level mountains or manipulate the weather if handled properly. In comic books, the hammer carries this inscription: "Whosoever holds this hammer, if he be worthy, shall possess the power of Thor."

The view of basic goodness is that we are all worthy. The weapon we wield is our speech. Like Mjölnir, our speech has incredible power. With a few words we can end a friendship. With a few others, we embark upon a business. Our speech is an extraordinarily potent tool and, like Thor, we have to wield it for the benefit of others, despite adversity.

When I was traveling for my first book, it seemed like there were two topics that everyone wanted to talk about. The first was sex. The second was difficult people. These two topics came up so frequently that I was tempted just to write another book entitled *Sex with Difficult People*.

However, when we got to discussing the topic of working with difficult people, it turned out to be anything but sexy. Difficulty in working with others often seems to stem from a breakdown in communication, particularly with individuals who feel that in order to be successful they need to put others down. At the heart of this type of speech is a sense of mindlessness. People get sloppy with communication and as a result cause harm.

When the Buddha began to attract followers, he realized that they would need some guidelines to govern their conduct so that the *sangha*, or community, would be harmonious. These guidelines are known as precepts; they were particular rules that the monks and nuns would adhere to in order to maintain virtuous conduct and prevent conflict.

The basic precepts were that monastics should not take life, not take what is not offered, not engage in sexual misconduct, not engage in mindless speech, and not ingest intoxicants. These precepts have been translated and interpreted across generations, and the basic ideas behind them still ring true today. One aspect of the mindless speech precept is that one should not engage in false speech. This includes lies, gossip and slander, harsh words, and even idle speech, the sort of talking you do just because there is an awkward silence or you feel uncomfortable. One translation of the precept reads:

> Aware of the suffering caused by unmindful speech, I vow to cultivate right speech. Knowing that words can create happiness or suffering, I will do my best to not lie, to not gossip or slander, to not use harsh or idle speech, and to not say things that bring about division or hatred. I aspire to always speak the truth.[2]

Can you imagine what a delightful work environment you would have if everyone committed to practicing mindful speech as articulated in this statement? Everyone would be aware that their very words have the potential to cause suffering or happiness for others and ideally would be more vigilant in choosing what to say. They would also pay more attention to what not to say and would refrain from putting others down, using profanity, or spreading gossip, lies, or negativity.

Deep Listening

The effects of practicing mindful speech are twofold. The first effect is that you cause less harm when you open your mouth.

The second effect is that you refrain from unnecessary speech, which leads to more opportunities to deeply listen to others. There is a Chinese proverb that says, "Two good talkers . . . not worth one good listener." If people put this proverb to work, you could have meetings where coworkers genuinely heard other people's opinions without getting defensive or coming up with ways to make themselves sound smarter. Overall, communication in the office, the field, the supermarket, everywhere would improve and people would become much more efficient in their roles.

Unfortunately, you cannot change the behavior of others; the only person you can change is yourself. In that sense, the first step in working with difficult people is to make sure you yourself are not acting like a difficult person. The act of listening is a solid safeguard against that.

One piece of advice passed on to me by a member of my sangha is that when in the midst of a difficult conversation, you should open yourself up by only asking questions. Refrain from trying to fix anything or solve the other person's issues. Just let their words wash over you like a wave, occasionally asking for clarification or more information. Doing so allows the other person to feel respected and heard. After listening deeply you may feel that you ought to offer your own two cents, but try to avoid doing so before you can see the situation clearly and understand the other person's point of view.

Deep listening is a skill set that we can develop over time in order to be mindful of our speech and compassionate in working with others. As the author Dr. Henry Cloud has said, "If we cannot communicate our listening in a way that lets the other person know that we have truly understood, empathy has not occurred."[3] Asking questions is one important way to let another person know that you are interested in connecting on an empathetic level. Taking this advice goes a long way in building genuine relationships.

MORE TOOLS FOR WORKING
WITH DIFFICULT PEOPLE

Of course, you can only listen and ask questions for so long. At some point, you may find that you need to speak up and participate in genuine communication with your coworkers. Shantideva, an Indian scholar and monk from the eighth century, is well known for proclaiming a text known as the *Bodhicharyavatara,* or *The Way of the Bodhisattva.*

The term *bodhisattva* comes from Sanskrit and can be broken down into its two halves. The first half, *bodhi,* can be translated as either "open" or "awake." *Sattva* means "being," as in an authentic human being. In other words, a bodhisattva is someone who bravely engages the world from the point of view of being supremely open and awake to whatever comes their way. Bodhisattvas manifest their basic goodness in a confident manner and are thus very successful when it comes to navigating through life. Typically, the bodhisattva is associated with the second of the three yanas of Buddhism: the Mahayana. That is because a bodhisattva goes well beyond their comfort level to exert themselves on behalf of others.

Shantideva knew that someone who wants to cultivate this point of view needs to use their speech as a weapon of delight, as opposed to one of aggression. While this is Mahayana activity, it is based in the Hinayana discipline of working on oneself. Because the yanas complement and interpenetrate, it is worth considering how our discipline of speech benefits ourselves while simultaneously affecting others. Shantideva said:

> When talking I should speak from my heart and on what
>   is relevant.
> Making the meaning clear and the speech pleasing
> I should not speak out of desire or hatred
> But in gentle tones and in moderation.[4]

If you aim to engage in a difficult conversation, the first step, Shantideva informs us, is to speak from your heart. Address the topic at hand in a clear and precise manner, without letting your emotions get in the way. If you can do that with gentleness, then the individuals you are working with may be able to truly hear your statement, regardless of whatever preconceived notions they may have.

Still, this is easier said than done. When you are sitting in a room full of jerks who are waiting for you to fail, your mind is likely not at ease. Shantideva has advice for this sort of situation as well:

And when your mind is wild or filled with mockery,
Or filled with pride and haughty arrogance,
Or when you would expose another's secret guilt,
To bring up old dissensions or to act deceitfully,
Or when you want to fish for praise,
Or criticize and spoil another's name,
Or use harsh language, sparring for a fight,
It's then that like a log you should remain.[5]

Here Shantideva lists a slew of obstacles that might come up when you're faced with difficult people. You might want to mock them, or think you are better than they are, or want to reveal their faults. When you notice those impulses arise, you should try to follow his advice and just come back to the present moment. You can just remain like a log. You can pause and come back to your breath. You can come back to what is in your heart and strive to speak from that perspective once more.

THE PATH OF MISTAKES

The fourth precept, the precept of mindful speech, is a ground for training. There will be times when you fail. During a presentation, you slip in an awkward comment that places blame on a coworker. Out to lunch with a friend, you let slip that you think Julie in accounting is having an affair. You may give up on listening to others or fire off your mouth.

Mistakes along the path are helpful. They are opportunities to reflect on the qualities that we long to cultivate, and to remember that it is only through practice that we create perfection. Even Thor has occasionally wielded Mjölnir in harmful ways; it does not mean he is any less worthy. Similarly, we cannot give up on mindful speech just because we make a mistake now and again.

The precepts are not fast and sturdy rules whereby you break one and are banished from Buddhism forever. Instead, they are guideposts for cultivating the aspects of ourselves that we long to cultivate. They are what we make of them, and part of that is recognizing that we mess up and reconciling that with our experience.

A few years ago, I was invited to begin volunteering at Reciprocity Foundation, a homeless aid organization in New York City, and eventually I joined their board. Many of the students the foundation serves are young, and when I was talking with one homeless youth about this idea of making mistakes, he brought up some advice his grandmother passed on to him: "Making one hundred different mistakes is progressive. Making one hundred of the same mistake is regressive."

In other words, if you make a mistake and accidentally gossip, or tell a white lie that comes back to bite you, learn from that experience. That is a valid training mechanism. However, if you continue to gossip and lie and learn nothing from the harm you are creating, you are backsliding on your spiritual path.

When making mistakes, the most important thing is to remember to be gentle with yourself. If you beat yourself up every time you say an unflattering word about a coworker, you are going to make yourself miserable. It is far better to acknowledge your mistake, vow to try not to repeat it, and maybe apologize or buy that person a cup of coffee some time.

On Matters of Small Concern

One of my former mentors has a wide variety of responsibilities ranging from international treaty negotiations to day-to-day minutiae in the nonprofit sector. I am always impressed by his ability to treat everyone he meets with as equally important. He might come to a meeting having just endured incredibly painful peace talks overseas and immediately get swooped up in a very minor drama. Instead of contextualizing it in the scheme of his overall work, he responds to every individual with respect. One of the most skillful things I have learned from him is that when you sit down with someone, you can treat them as the most important person in your life for those few moments.

Hagakure is a text composed by Yamamoto Tsunetomo, a samurai turned Zen priest who lived in the eighteenth century. It is an excellent work, offering pith instructions that are still relevant today. One piece of advice reads:

> Among the maxims on Lord Naoshige's wall there was this one: "Matters of great concern should be treated lightly." Master Ittei commented, "Matters of small concern should be treated seriously."[6]

A few years ago, I served as the interim director of a nonprofit. The board of trustees had dissolved, the previous director had left abruptly, and the staff was freaking out. After reflecting deeply on the example set by my mentor and this basic tenet offered by Tsunetomo, I met with the finance manager, who broke down the quarterly budget in no uncertain terms: we needed to raise a large amount of funds or shut down shop. Immediately after that, I met with the facilities manager, a very sweet and thoughtful individual who really felt the most important thing for the organization at that time was to switch to a new type of trash bag that would be less harmful to the environment.

In that moment, telling him that the trash bags didn't matter in the scheme of things would have been demoralizing for us both. I decided to take a different approach, one that was not based in fear of running out of money or accomplishing my long to-do list to right the organization. For the half hour we met, I just really listened to the facilities manager and learned more about trash bags than I ever expected to in this lifetime.

At the end of the meeting, he was appreciative. "I know there is a lot going on right now, but this had actually been bugging me for months. I just appreciate that you listened to me and are supporting me." We have been close ever since, because I took what seemed a small concern at the time and treated it seriously.

When someone comes to you with an issue, they often believe it is the most important thing on your agenda as well as theirs. To treat it as otherwise is a slap in the face. To lean in and meet that person in that state of mind where they can sense that you value what they are working on is a gift. When you create this kind of space for someone, they will often resolve a difficult issue in an amicable way, because you offered them your heart.

When we engage our speech in a kind and mindful manner, we are not just avoiding causing harm to others. We are treating every encounter with our coworkers as a spiritual practice, an opportunity to connect with our goodness and theirs. Like Thor with his hammer, we have the ability to wield our speech as an instrument for good, based in the idea that we are worthy and capable enough to overcome all adversity. The more we engage in this attitude of basic goodness and treating others as worthy, the more we will inspire them to join us in attempting to create a better work environment and a better society.

5 / RUSSIAN ROULETTE AND THE POWER OF JUST DO IT

My friend Marina is a good nurse. For some reason, I just know it. I have never seen her in the emergency room, but she is heavily courted by various hospitals and private practices, and her calm demeanor with tough issues assures me of this fact. One day I asked her what she thinks makes her good in a crisis. She said, "I just have to perform, so I do."

I think many of us have had similar experiences when presented with challenges either at work or in our personal lives. Often it is not the best-trained or most highly educated people who succeed; it's the people who are present enough in a situation to do what simply needs to be done.

A common saying in the Shambhala Buddhist tradition is that simple can understand complicated but complicated cannot understand simple. The point is that if you can slow down and be present enough, you can simplify even the most convoluted situation. However, if you walk into a complicated situation with a complicated mind, it may turn out that you continue to perpetuate trouble. Furthermore, someone who has a very set, opinionated mind may not perceive a situation clearly and will not be able to figure out simple solutions.

The tricky thing, then, if we want to be successful at work, is to figure out how to be simple. *Simple* is a word that I think has a negative connotation in our society; you may think I am asking you to be dumb. Simple here is the opposite of dumb; it is being present enough to see the brilliance available in any situation.

In the traditional Buddhist point of view, it is said that we habitually see our world through three different lenses: passion, aggression, and ignorance. Passion may manifest in a variety of ways: as greed, jealousy, lust, or longing. Anger may come forth as hatred, frustration, or impatience. Ignorance may show up as bias, avoidance, or fear. Whatever we experience on or off the meditation cushion can be traced back to these three root poisons. It's a bit of a game of Russian roulette as to which emotional response we use to address the people and issues that come up in our life.

The unfortunate thing is that, for most of us, the game is rigged because the gun we are using has a bullet in each chamber: either a passion bullet, an aggression bullet, or an ignorance bullet. We pick up this gun hundreds of times a day and put it to our head, holding ourselves hostage to these emotional reactions. We pull the trigger, hoping nothing will happen, but we end up shooting ourselves full of one of these three root emotions.

This is not to say that emotions are bad. Emotions are awesome. When we feel true love for someone, we feel uplifted. When we feel real sadness, our tears can be authentic expressions of it that are cathartic. However, most of us do not feel our emotions fully, letting them come up and roll across our minds. Most of us end up sinking our teeth into the story lines that come with these emotions, constantly thinking about what happened or what we can do in the future to prevent our feelings of upset. In other words, we are not present enough to feel our emotions fully and instead get hooked by them, attached to them, and that causes us suffering.

In the workplace, this may play out in different ways. For example, you may desire someone else's role or salary, and fixating on that desire may cause you to suffer. Or you may feel aggression toward your coworkers because they are not pulling their weight on a shared project, and the heat from that anger keeps you up at night. Or you may experience boredom, a sense of aloofness; you don't even care about the project at hand, so you phone it in and get in trouble for a shoddy performance.

It is no surprise that after years or decades of indulging these three basic emotional states, we fall prey to them very easily. The purpose of meditation practice is to allow us to unhinge the bear traps of passion, aggression, and ignorance and to yank ourselves free and into the present moment.

Even if you're not formally meditating, you can still apply the basic technique of shamatha when you are at work and notice that you are drifting off into one of these three realms. You can leave a note for yourself somewhere on your desk or computer that simply reads *Thinking*. When you catch yourself getting lost in a fantasy or strong emotional state, you can remind yourself that you ought to be focusing on your work, and come back to your breath for a moment before returning to being present with the task at hand.

The more you are able to be present, the better you will be able to handle tough situations when they arise at work. I believe that is what makes Marina a good nurse. Chögyam Trungpa Rinpoche seems to agree here, as he once said, "When you're in the middle of a situation, you automatically pick up on what is needed. It's not a question of how to do it—you just do it."[1]

This idea of "just do it" was picked up on some time ago by Nike. In the commercials for their shoes, however, they seem to imply that only through the speed provided by their product can you accomplish what you seek to achieve.

The Buddhist view is not that we should just act on whatever whim or fancy catches our spirit; instead, when faced with a difficult scenario, we should come back to the present moment, right now, and then act from a place of mindfulness. Just doing something, and doing it properly, comes from slowing down rather than speeding up. When you are caught in the immediacy of a situation and can be present with your own mind, you will act skillfully in a natural manner. This is the antithesis of Nike's message.

In his book *The Shambhala Principle*, Sakyong Mipham Rinpoche writes, "Every moment has its energy; either it will ride us, or we can ride it."[2] Entering into a difficult situation, you can either get swept up in the momentum of passion, aggression, and ignorance or you can come into the present moment and take charge of the scenario with mindfulness, simply paying attention to what is going on right now.

Chögyam Trungpa Rinpoche, in his seminars on work, sex, and money, said, "Now is all the time, and it is choiceless. . . . Work takes place now." When faced with a difficult task, we really have no choice but to address it from the perspective of now. That is where work resides—in the present moment. If we hope to be able to address the conflicts and challenges that arise at work, that is where we need to meet them.

Unfortunately, this is not easy. When a major upset occurs, people either try to solve the problem immediately, try to blame someone for it, or try to run from it. These are those three basic responses at work again: we get hooked by the desire to eliminate the problem, we use aggression to place blame, or we try to ignore it. Once we fall prey to this approach, it is hard to break that pattern.

The hardest thing I have learned in approaching difficult situations is that sometimes the best thing to do is nothing at all. Sometimes we need to create space around difficulty in order for solutions to arise. When we take a step back from a problem, that simple mind that arises can unravel the complicated situation. The more space we create for ourselves and others, the more clearly we are able to see a situation.

This is why the training in meditation practice is so important. When you sit down to meditate, you are training yourself in resting in space. Instead of holding the gun of passion/aggression/ignorance to your own head, you are placing it down on the ground, over and over again. You see that holding yourself hostage to these emotional states causes you to suffer, and you vow to try to free yourself.

This may be the most important thing we can do to prepare ourselves for suffering, in or out of the workplace. The more we can safeguard our mind by placing that gun down on the ground, the fewer external factors will hold sway over us. Shantideva, our dear friend from the previous chapter, has advice on this particular issue:

> My property, my honor—all can freely go,
> My body and my livelihood as well.
> And even other virtues may decline,
> But never will I let my mind regress.[3]

Here Shantideva points out a basic Buddhist truth: that all things are impermanent and subject to change. You cannot cling to external factors like your property or your honor, which are guaranteed to come and go. Even your body and your livelihood are subject to the simple truth of change. All the various aspects of your life may ebb and flow over time, but that does not mean that you cannot safeguard your awake mind in the midst of that process.

The most important thing you can do for yourself is to practice coming back to the present, over and over again. If you can retain a fluid and flexible mind, you are less likely to become attached to passion, aggression, and ignorance when working with external factors.

This spacious and flexible mind is something we all have the ability to cultivate. It is not something you need to study in school or learn in an expensive training program. You can cultivate it through meditation practice in your own home, in your own time, on a daily basis. Similarly, you don't have to base your success at work on how many hours you have logged, or how quick you are at accomplishing certain tasks, or how much money you make. Instead, you can pride yourself on being spacious and not constantly engaging in Russian roulette with the loaded gun of strong emotions. It is up to you to determine your personal measure for success.

In a teaching on work, sex, and money, Chögyam Trungpa Rinpoche said, "These days, people sometimes say they can't do certain work because they haven't taken a course in it. A lot of things in life don't have to be taught in courses. . . .You just need to drop your hesitation and use your intelligence. You need to get into it and just do it."[4] Granted, if you are a brain surgeon, you need extensive training. But when you have trained yourself well in meditation, you can just act in accordance with the situation at hand and do it.

We always have the option to just do it. We always have the ability to rest in spacious mind in order to make sure we are skillful in our actions. We always can put down the gun of passion, aggression, and ignorance and instead offer ourselves, as we are, knowing that through slowing down and offering space we can just do anything.

6 / FIVE SLOGANS FOR CHANGING HOW YOU VIEW WORK

Whether you are trying to determine what you want to do for your livelihood or trying to figure out how to bring your meditation practice into your livelihood, how you view what you do is important. Knowing your own intention behind what you do is the difference between schlepping through your life and living a life with meaning.

After discussing the power of intention in chapter 1, we explored the Buddhist notion of basic goodness, or our inherent worthiness. Touching this innate aspect of who we are empowers us to bring about great success in all of our endeavors. From there, we looked at the idea of right livelihood and how we can map that out so that this term has meaning for us in today's world.

In the vein of not causing harm as we engage in this process, we saw that we can wield our speech as a weapon for good and that if we are able to allow space in our work life, then we can produce success instead of being yanked about by passion, aggression, and ignorance.

In some sense, these principles are just the beginning of connecting our work life with the Hinayana path. The Hinayana is a path of not creating harm and trying to become familiar with yourself as you explore your world. It is a path of really working with your own mind and heart so that you can see how you suffer and, ideally, stop doing that so much.

Atisha Dipamkara Shrijnana was a master in the Kadampa school of Tibetan Buddhism. He is said to have lived from 982 to 1054 and taught extensively during a time in Tibet that was marked by political and social unrest. He is widely credited with popularizing and systematizing the *lojong* teachings of Buddhism.

Lo can be translated from the Tibetan as "mind" and *jong* as "training." Prior to Atisha, these teachings on training the mind were held closely by the monastic tradition, but he saw how relevant they are to lay practitioners and made them broadly available. These teachings are, in some sense, our first venture into the Mahayana path, one aspect of which is taking others' success and happiness as a basis for our own joy.

Today, there are fifty-nine lojong slogans, and many scholars have written commentaries on them. But the Buddha did not lay out teachings and say, "Please, take my word for it. Do as I say, and you'll get enlightened. Trust me." Instead, it is said that the initial words he uttered to his first students were, "Come and see for yourself."

With this invitation in mind, we can explore the lojong teachings, and all Buddhist teachings, with an uncluttered mind and heart. We can investigate not just what has traditionally been said about them, but what they actually mean to us and how they can affect our life. Doing so keeps the Buddha's teachings fresh and relevant; it is a living, breathing set of teachings as opposed to strict dogma that we must adhere to. If there is something in this book, or any book that discusses Buddhism, that you try out and feel is not valid in your experience, then you ought to discard it.

Five of these mind training slogans that Atisha documented I think are particularly relevant to our endeavor of bringing mindfulness and discipline off the meditation cushion and into our place of work.

Of the two witnesses, hold the principal one.

This slogan highlights the notion that at the core of who we are, we are worthy. We are capable. As a result of developing confidence in our own basic goodness, we have deep trust in ourselves. When tricky situations arise (and in my experience, they often do), there can be multiple points of view as to what has happened or what should happen. That is what Atisha means when he points out that there are two witnesses—there is other people's view of you and your actions and your own view of yourself. Of those two points of view, the principal one is your own insight.

Meditation practice is a practice in getting to know yourself very well. No one has spent more time with you than you. You are your own best adviser. Because you know yourself well, you ought to respect your own insight and listen to it. Trust your intuition, and lead from that perspective.

Don't ponder others.

When we obsess over other people's actions or affairs, we are not bettering anyone. Traleg Kyabgon Rinpoche has commented on this slogan in his book *The Practice of Lojong*, saying, "When we think about others, we usually concentrate on their problems and defects."[1] That is clearly a waste of time, and any satisfaction we may gain from dwelling on other people's faults is temporary and can leave a sour taste in our mouth.

This means that you should not take delight in other people's misfortunes or waste your time fantasizing about what may or may not be happening with them. Obsessing over other people's business perpetuates inner gossip, ruining your mindfulness.

From the perspective of mindful speech, one could argue that the moment you begin pondering things about others out loud to coworkers, you are beginning to gossip about them. There is being inquisitive, asking why someone did a certain thing or how they are attempting to tackle a project, and then there is pondering their faults aloud.

As always, the difference comes down to what view you hold as you approach the other person. If you can keep a fresh state of mind, then you may be open to what they have to say. If you are coming at this individual with the idea that they are likely in the wrong, then you may already be pondering their affairs in a negative way.

Traleg Rinpoche goes on to say, "Wasting time speculating about other people's affairs can be toxic and self-destructive." It does not do you any good to ponder others; it can only create harm for yourself.

Don't bring things to a painful point.

This slogan is one of my favorites. How often have you wanted to get in the last word or tried to alleviate your discomfort by forcing an issue beyond what another person felt able to discuss? When we engage in simple acts like this in an attempt to bring ourselves comfort, we are actually doing the opposite: we are bringing things to a painful point.

Another way we bring things to a painful point is by running away from topics that scare us. It could be your finances, the death of a loved one, or just your own insecurity in not knowing what you ought to be doing with your life. When you feel the tug of discomfort, you may want to shut down and not deal with these issues. You might lock yourself up in your room and watch multiple seasons of *Game of Thrones*, or go out drinking excessively, or spend hours obsessively checking out your favorite Web sites.

Unfortunately, when we hide from our problems, they tend to get bigger. When you come out of your room or that bar or that discount clothing site, the same issues you may have thought would have gone away are only more in your face. As a result, this avoidance tactic—or any disingenuous effort to shy away from discomfort—is likely to only cause more pain. Instead of avoiding discomfort, you can lean into your life and tackle difficult topics straightforwardly and mindfully.

This is not to say that you should never give space to difficult topics, as was discussed in the previous chapter. Sometimes the most skillful thing to do is give a tricky situation a lot of space and let it resolve itself. However, if you find that you are avoiding something, you ought to practice meditation, bring yourself fully into the present, become familiar with your own sense of spaciousness, and act from that point of view. Doing so allows you to avoid bringing things to a painful point.

Don't be swayed by external circumstances.

As someone who is trying to bridge the seemingly large gap between your spiritual life and your work life, you should practice mindfulness whenever and wherever possible, not just when it feels good. Traleg Rinpoche has made the point that if you train to be present and spacious only when things are good, you will feel that way only when things are good. When things are difficult, you will not be able to experience the qualities you are trying to cultivate.

Chögyam Trungpa Rinpoche has also commented on this slogan, saying, "Although your external circumstances may vary, your practice should not be dependent on that."[2] So please do not think of your meditation practice as something that happens for a few minutes here and there throughout your day but something that you can continuously engage in, especially when times get tough.

Don't expect applause.

The reason we try to bring our meditation practice and our livelihood together is not to attain great fame but because it is a way to live our life with meaning. If you go about your work—

or your meditation—hoping that someone will say how accomplished you are, you will end up disappointed. Instead, relax your expectations. If you can do that, then when someone does praise you for your good work, you will likely feel delighted.

Pema Chödrön has commented on this slogan, saying, "We can thank others, but we should give up all hope of getting thanked back. Simply keep the door open without expectations."[3] In other words, just because we shouldn't expect applause does not mean we should not applaud others. Taking delight in others' good work is a gift to ourselves, as well as an act of kindness to the object of our admiration.

Similarly, if you engage in your work or your practice with enthusiasm, mindfulness, and spaciousness, not only will you become more efficient, but you will enjoy it much more. That is its own reward.

I once asked my friend Erin about the most important piece of advice someone had offered her about her work life. She admitted to a tendency to be pretty hard on herself and said that the best advice she had ever received is that no one is going to pat you on the back for not taking care of yourself. So to invert this traditional lojong slogan, you can also remember the importance of gentleness and taking care of yourself.

I would say that these slogans conclude our exploration of the first of the three vehicles of the Buddhist path, but in some sense it is only the beginning. As I mentioned, these slogans are typically associated with the Mahayana teachings of Tibetan Buddhism, which emphasize working with (and for) others as part of our spiritual journey.

The path of exploring the dharma is a lifelong one. The idea of determining who you want to be when you grow up is a constantly changing process, as I doubt any of us truly ever feels we have, officially, "grown up." We are forever growing, and, as a result, we must continuously return to these fundamental teachings on discovering our evolving intention, deepening trust in our basic goodness, becoming inquisitive about our life and livelihood, and engaging our speech and activity in a spacious and mindful manner. If we train in these basic tasks, we will see success in our work and live a life that is meaningful and in line with who we want to be.

PART TWO

MAHAYANA
On-the-Job Compassion

7 / ROM-COMS, ZOMBIES, AND BODHICITTA

Our whole job is to relate to people.

—*Sakyong Mipham Rinpoche*

I am the first to admit that I enjoy a good romantic comedy. Even with the predictable plot twists and cheesy writing, I can still get into just about anything in that movie genre. My favorite is *Love Actually*. The opening scene takes place in Heathrow Airport, where there are multiple shots of reunions as people greet their loved ones. Over these images Hugh Grant speaks about how whenever he feels despair at the state of the world, he thinks about the arrivals terminal and the pure, uncomplicated love that permeates that environment.

There is something in scenes like this one that is easy to identify with. We have all been in that situation, awaiting someone's arrival or rushing to see someone we care for, and then they appear and our heart feels lifted up, we feel lighter, and in that moment we are not thinking about our own myriad of problems. Those moments, when we are able to transcend being a head case and relax to the point where we are not thinking solely about ourselves, feel wonderful.

This basic experience of opening up beyond just thinking about *me* and *my problems* is the basis of the Mahayana, or greater vehicle. Traditionally speaking, it is said to be greater because it transcends working just for your own benefit; it is based in taking others' happiness as the source of your own. It is a path of stepping beyond yourself and being completely available to the world, living your life in a way that is not only meaningful to you but serves others as well. The first step on that path is discovering how you suffer and learning to be empathetic when others suffer in the same ways.

ACKNOWLEDGING SUFFERING

The Buddha taught extensively about how we suffer. He said that we are, in fact, trapped in a constant cycle of suffering, known as samsara. *Samsara* is a Sanskrit term that describes the continuous flow of the pain of our existence from birth until death and into birth again.

Samsara includes that itchiness we feel on the meditation cushion, that longing to leap off it, that discomfort we feel sitting still with our own mind. It is the full range of pains that are inherent in birth, aging, sickness, and death. It is the loaded gun that we hold to our head, full of passion, aggression, and ignorance. It is the fact that we cling so tightly to our set opinions and expectations that we leave little room in our mind to enjoy what is actually occurring right now.

The interesting thing is that you have certainly already glimpsed this cycle of suffering while on the meditation cushion. You may have sat down one day to meditate and immediately begun playing out a scenario at work. Your recent project went well, and everyone is cheering you and lifting you in the air, you are a hero. You might spend a good deal of time letting your mind run wild with that idea. Then all of a sudden doubt creeps in, and you think, "What if I actually fail? What if I blow it?" Your mind flees to images of being chewed out by your boss, getting fired, clearing out your desk. Minutes later you are mentally living on unemployment and never hearing back from potential job prospects.

We all fall victim to this game of hope and fear. We seek pleasure and want to avoid pain. We yearn for praise and abhor blame. We fantasize about fame but fear disgrace. We desire gain and are terrified of loss. In the Buddhist canon, these four contrasting pairs are referred to as the eight worldly dharmas.

One summer I was living in Ithaca, New York, and would attend teachings at the Dalai Lama's monastery there. Some of the monks who gave talks were very new to America and had not learned the ins and outs of the English language. I remember one monk giving a talk on the eight worldly dharmas. He said, "When you give in to these eight, you will walk around like a zombie."

"A zombie," I thought. "That's interesting; you're just aimlessly wandering through life."

"A zombie," he said. "You know, an undead person who eats brains!"

In my own experience, when you are attached to the eight worldly dharmas, constantly basing your happiness on hoping for positive things and fearing that they will not arise, you go through life in a listless fashion. You are like a zombie in that you are going through your day wrapped up in your own head, not really paying attention to the people around you.

The more you meditate, though, the more likely you are to notice the way your mind slips into these eight worldly dharmas, and the more likely you are to come back to the present moment. You become very familiar with your own habitual patterns, and as a result it becomes easier to catch yourself when you spiral into one of them. You begin to have some basic mastery over your mental state and are not as easily lured into this cycle of suffering.

THE PATH OF THE BODHISATTVA

When you become familiar with how you get hooked by suffering, you begin to recognize the same sort of habitual reactions taking place with other people. You begin to realize that you are not the only one who gets yanked into the game of hope and fear. We all suffer. The fact that you see more clearly how you get hooked by suffering only highlights how your friends and coworkers are going through the exact same thing.

At this point in your spiritual journey, you begin to comprehend that this whole meditation thing is not just about you. It's about helping others so that they aren't so hooked by their own pain and drama. This is not a matter of proselytizing, where we have to spread the good word about mindfulness in order to save everyone. It's just the fact that our heart begins to open up to others as we realize that we are all just striving to be happy.

When you see how others suffer, just like you, your heart goes out to them. This is the blossoming of *bodhicitta*. It is like that moment in the airport, when for a second you drop all thoughts about self-protection and instead allow your heart to be completely vulnerable. You might become very tender and aware of your environment, and that is a wonderful feeling. You are allowing yourself to open up to the world, and find that your heart has the capacity to embrace it all.

Bodhicitta is a Sanskrit term. *Bodhi* has the same meaning as in *bodhisattva:* "open" or "awake." *Citta* can be translated as "heart" or "mind." There is not a lot of difference between the heart and the mind in the Sanskrit. Putting these two terms together, you can think of bodhicitta as that experience of opening your heart, or being awake enough to allow your heart to be available to any experience, good or bad.

We always have the capacity to open our heart in this way. To do so is the foundation of the Mahayana path. We are dropping our set concepts of who we are, or who we ought to be, and are experiencing reality as it is in the moment. The more you are able to open yourself to the world, the more you will be able to ride the waves of your life in a way that brings you joy.

A being who practices the path of bodhicitta is referred to as a bodhisattva. As mentioned before, a bodhisattva is a brave individual who continuously offers this sense of openness in order to be more fully connected to their world and to benefit others in the process.

In the *Naga King Anavatapta-Requested Sutra* it is said, "A bodhisattva who possesses one quality holds all the excellent qualities of the Buddhas. What is that one quality? A mind which does not forsake anyone from one's heart."[1] While that is a bold statement to make, this is the practice of the bodhisattva—opening your heart fully to everyone, the people you love and the people who annoy the heck out of you. When you are able to do that, you grow as a human being and create positive change in the world.

Opening our heart in this unconditional, vulnerable way actually makes us stronger. It shifts our whole way of thinking. We begin to realize that we actually experience a more tenacious form of happiness in thinking about others before ourselves. As Chögyam Trungpa Rinpoche once said, "The starting point of relative bodhicitta practice is realizing that others could actually be more important than ourselves."[2] This is a big shift in view! If we can adapt to the idea that others are actually more important than ourselves, we may find that we are less in our head and more available to our world.

The funny thing is, when we make this shift from thinking only about ourselves to thinking of others, we do experience joy. Recently I was out for a run with my friend Sara. I had been staying with her for a week, and she also had a friend visiting from Australia, who seemed immensely cheerful all the time. I asked Sara why she thought her friend was so jovial. "She's so great!" Sara said. "All week she has been smiling and just doing all sorts of things to help out. She is just one of those people who have zero hesitancy in being helpful." That is the mark of a bodhisattva, I think.

A bodhisattva is someone who acts in a way that is skillful, even before action is requested. Bodhisattvas lean into their world and are present enough in the moment that they can do whatever is needed. Furthermore, they experience joy from being this helpful. They see the delight that comes from helping others and find that doing so brings them happiness as well.

In that sense, opening your heart to others is the best kind of double-edged sword. You are cutting through your own stuck mind-set, moving beyond just thinking of yourself. At the same time, you are cutting through others' difficulties and being helpful in a way that brings everyone contentment.

When you offer your heart, you are also more in tune with your world. You get a larger perspective because you are not thinking solely about yourself. You are able to soak in the brilliance of your environment and experience your life fully. You are available to offer yourself, all of yourself. Whatever difficulties may arise, you always have the ability to tap into this open-hearted state, this bodhicitta, and act in accordance with whatever needs to happen.

Opening your heart and making yourself vulnerable in this way is a scary thing to do. In today's fast-paced work environment, people do not always see vulnerability as something positive. It is perceived as a weakness rather than a strength. Traditional texts state the opposite, though: they say that bodhicitta actually gives you incredible strength that, when realized, can overcome even the toughest of obstacles.

Take a moment to think of a leader you admire. It could be a mentor, a celebrity, a politician, or someone active in your community. Now think of the qualities that you think make them a strong leader. Has there ever been a time when that individual let you see a spot of doubt? Did they ever profess something about their personal life or let you in on a mistake they had made and told you how they dealt with it? Likely they did, at some point. These little moments of vulnerability are not signs of weakness to many of us, but signs that someone is human. They are signs that they are like us, and thus worthy of our empathy.

I worked for a few months as a field organizer for the Obama presidential reelection campaign. After the race was won, I was surprised to see our president exhibit his vulnerable side. During a speech in which he addressed his entire staff, he reflected back to when he was our age, working in a similar position as a community organizer in the South Side of Chicago.

He began by saying how much better organized and more efficient we were than he was, and how even if he had not won reelection, he would still have had hope for the future because of the many people on his campaign who had developed into future leaders for America. As he went on to say how proud he was of us, tears began to roll down his face. It was a moment of connection for thousands of us on staff, seeing this man who is so powerful express that power through a moment of complete vulnerability.

It is said that people are more likely to follow a leader if that individual is easy to relate to in some way. We are inspired by leaders who make themselves available. In his book *Integrity*, Dr. Henry Cloud wrote, "The tension between vulnerability and strength in leaders cannot be lost." This is the power of bodhicitta. It is not a weepy heart or a heart that whines a lot. It has tremendous strength because it is a heart that is open, capable, and brave.

When faced with cynicism or overt threats, a strong leader will rise to the occasion with a sense of openness. I am a firm believer that cynicism can be overcome by the power of an awake heart and that uncomfortable conversations can be softened through bodhicitta. I believe that whatever life throws at us, we can meet it with vulnerability and strength simultaneously, if we dare to tread on the bodhisattva's path.

Not unlike Hugh Grant in *Love Actually*, you can snap yourself out of whatever gloomy despair you may feel about the state of the world or your own personal situation. You can tread the Mahayana path to benefit yourself and others simultaneously. You can access bodhicitta, a pure, uncomplicated source of love, and offer that to the world. I'm a firm believer that bodhicitta is the remedy this world needs.

8 / MENTORS AND VIRTUE

When in reliance on someone your defects wane
And your positive qualities grow like the waxing moon,
To cherish such a spiritual friend more than your own body
Is the practice of a Bodhisattva.[1]

—*Ngulchu Thogme*

Virtue is a term that is often misunderstood in the Western world. If you pick up the *Oxford English Dictionary,* you will see it defined as "behavior showing high moral standards." From a Buddhist perspective, virtue is slightly different. It is not based in contemporary moral standards, which, like everything else, are impermanent and subject to change over time. Instead, it refers to a bodhisattva's ability to know what aspects of life to engage in and which to refrain from.

Virtue, or *gewa* in Tibetan, is about listening to and leading from your bodhicitta. You can align yourself with your open heart and let that be your moral compass. The Tibetan Buddhist teacher Tsoknyi Rinpoche once wrote, "Gewa means making choices that extend our emotional and intellectual strength, illuminate our potential greatness, build our confidence, and enhance our ability to assist those in need of help."[2] Virtue, then, is about flexing our bodhicitta muscles.

We are strengthening our resolve to offer an open heart, which shows off our potential, deepens our faith in our goodness, and allows us to actually change our work situation for the better. Virtue, in this sense, is about tuning in fully to your open heart and acting in a way that is in accordance with whatever your inner voice is telling you.

Virtue is also connected to discernment. For example, you could be out with coworkers at a bar and you notice that Matt, the office gossip, starts steering the conversation toward the zone of complaining about your boss. Intuitively you know that engaging him in this conversation might end up causing trouble for you. Yet you do it, and the next day, word has gotten around that you have some serious beef with your boss. If this happens consistently over time, you begin to discern that maybe Matt isn't the best company to keep.

Similarly, you may have another coworker, Miranda, whom you can sit down with and in a half hour you will have fed each other's creativity to the point of solving a long agenda of issues. Between the two of you, fresh solutions naturally arise. You walk away from that encounter feeling refreshed, knowing that you want to spend more time working with Miranda.

One aspect of discernment is learning what company you want to keep. Matt, our office gossip, may burn us a few times before we realize that maybe we should not hang out with him so much. Miranda, our creative colleague, is someone we might even want to go into business with some day. It is through being present and open that we begin to notice whom we want to spend our time with and our energy on. We begin to discern how we can live a life of virtue, based in bodhicitta.

Ngulchu Thogme was a meditation master in the fourteenth century. His text *The Thirty-Seven Practices of a Bodhisattva* is full of pith instructions for how to live a life based in connecting with your own bodhicitta. In the verse that opens this chapter, he instructs us in the qualities of a true spiritual friend. According to Ngulchu Thogme, if you are spending time with someone and your negative qualities start to wane while your positive qualities blossom, then you have found someone worth spending time with. Doing so is virtuous activity.

This person doesn't have to be a meditation teacher or even a coworker. One day I was walking down the street with a former girlfriend, and she turned to me and said out of the blue, "You know, I think I've become nicer in the years since we started dating." I reflected on that, touched, and responded, "You know, I think I've gotten kinder too." It was a very tender moment, recognizing that just by spending time together we had encouraged each other's positive qualities.

In traveling for my first book and preparing to write this one, I began asking everyone I met about the idea of a spiritual friend in the office. Think for a moment if you already have one. Is there someone with whom you naturally feel an affinity? Do you encourage one another? Do you rise above office pettiness and talk about topics that are meaningful to you? If so, you have discovered a rare gift and can follow Ngulchu Thogme's advice by cherishing them dearly.

Mentors as Spiritual Friends

Often, the role of spiritual friend is filled by someone you can look up to as a mentor. I think mentors are incredibly important. I have had several in my own life. For my managerial and operations work, I was lucky to learn from people who were both well established in the worldly sense and also strong Buddhist practitioners. For my writing, I have come to rely on fellow authors who offer me advice on navigating the publishing industry. For my meditation practice, I have my root teacher, Sakyong Mipham Rinpoche, and have had the good fortune to have established relationships with many other teachers in the Tibetan Buddhist tradition. I believe that I owe whatever knowledge I have to my mentors.

In conversations about mentors, my peers have pointed out that we often don't go looking for them; we just stumble across the right person. Often we are attracted to someone because we admire what it is they are doing and long to connect with that individual. From there, we form a relationship and gradually come to trust the other person. The other person, in some sense, proves that they are virtuous, that they have been discerning in a way that we would like to cultivate, and as a result we begin to ask their advice. Some people turn to their mentors for guidance in making transitions, others for help with research, and others for connections to jobs or positions. Whatever advice it may be, we are trusting in our own discernment as well as our mentor's.

Interestingly enough, I have found that individuals who have a strong relationship to a mentor have seriously contemplated where they will be and what they will be doing in five to ten years. There is something about having such a spiritual friend that inspires you to think beyond your immediate situation. You are able to discern what aspects of your life you want to cultivate and to expand on them within a supportive relationship.

WORKING FOR THE HAPPINESS OF OTHERS

Virtue, however, involves more than just being discerning about the company you keep. It is also about exerting yourself on behalf of others. Our old friend Shantideva has several verses on this topic, starting with this one:

> With perfect and unyielding faith,
> With steadfastness, respect, and courtesy,
> With modesty and conscientiousness,
> Work calmly for the happiness of others.[3]

It is important that in the company we keep and the actions we perform, we hold the view that we are working for the happiness of others as well as ourselves. With that in mind, Shantideva explains a number of ways to cultivate virtue in the context of our livelihood.

First, we can develop deep faith. Faith, in this case, is not saying you should trust a benign deity to bless you with a perfect plan. Instead, it is faith in your own basic goodness. It is faith in your own ability to develop the presentations you need to develop, lead the teams you need to lead, and cultivate your career path as you would like. Virtue, in this case, is partly about developing perfect and unyielding faith in yourself.

Shantideva mentions several other qualities related to the development of virtue: You can be steadfast in your devotion to connecting with bodhicitta and working for others. You can have respect and common courtesy for your coworkers. You can exhibit modesty and act in a humble manner, even when praised or promoted. Last but not least, you can be conscientious in all your activity, discerning whether it is helpful or harmful to your place of employment, be it a warehouse, a coffee shop, or even a publishing house.

Furthermore, we should do all of this calmly. Virtue is not about trying to be the sharpest, the smartest, or the quickest employee. It is about coming into the present moment and connecting with your heart in a way that is of benefit. Chögyam Trungpa Rinpoche said, "There is often a misunderstanding or confusion between accomplishment and speed."[4] He went on to point out that it is often those who work tirelessly, consistently, but slowly who accomplish the most—not the people who were the most frantic in their endeavors or the best at multitasking.

SLOW AND STEADY WINS THE RACE

I was asked once on a radio show what I thought was the biggest obstacle today for people who are interested in meditation. I said that, in my opinion, it's the fact that we live in an incredibly speedy world where great value is placed in accomplishing things quickly rather than well. We are also accustomed to instant gratification. If you want something these days, you don't have to go out and look very far for it. In fact, you don't even have to leave your home; you can order almost anything online and have it mailed to you. In New York City, you can even order groceries online, including fresh vegetables and fruit, and have it all delivered to your door from a business called Fresh Direct.

However, if you are expecting instant gratification when it comes to your meditation practice, you will end up sorely disappointed. There's no Fresh Direct option for your practice. If you are seeking a sense of peaceful abiding, it doesn't happen after twenty minutes of meditation. It's a gradual process, and it can be months or years before you notice a marked change in your experience. In fact, that marked change may very well end up being that you are kinder, or gentler, or more in touch with your bodhicitta.

The same principle of gradual development can be applied to cultivating virtue. If you have been living your life without much discernment, you can't just sit down for a few minutes to meditate and then immediately know who you should be hanging out with and who you should cut out of your life. Acknowledging the choice to act in a virtuous way is just the first step on a very long journey to actualizing those decisions.

It takes an incredible amount of time and conscientiousness to deepen your resolve to live a virtuous life. That is why you have to be patient with yourself and attempt to work around the clock on engaging in virtue. When it comes to living a virtuous life and still accomplishing a great deal at work, slow and steady wins the race.

In *Hagakure*, it is said, "A retainer is a man who remains consistently undistracted twenty-four hours a day, whether he is in the presence of his master or in public. If one is careless during his rest period, the public will see him as being only careless."[5] In other words, if you are attempting to cultivate virtue in your life, the simplest way to do it is not to drop your virtuous activity at the door when you clock out at work. Whether you are at work or out with friends or arguing with your spouse, you should still practice virtue. Otherwise, you will be perceived as careless, if not by others, then at least by your own self.

EXERCISE FOR CULTIVATING VIRTUE

I recommend taking some time to contemplate what virtue means to you and how you might cultivate it throughout your day. To begin, you can practice shamatha meditation for five to ten minutes.

After sitting for this brief period and feeling grounded, contemplate a simple question: On a scale of one to ten, with one being "never ever" and ten being "all day long," how much of my day do I spend cultivating virtue? See what number arises, and if that feels like a genuine answer.

Having contemplated that question, ask yourself, "What would it look like if I moved that number a step up the scale toward ten?" What would change in your life if you were to practice virtue more consistently throughout your day? Would you treat certain people differently?

Once more, ask, "What would it look like if I moved that number a step up the scale toward ten?" What aspects of your life would you cultivate more? Which would you choose to cut out?

After a few minutes of contemplation, come back to shamatha. Rest your mind on your breath, and relax.

You can connect with the potency of your open heart in any moment, and from that perspective you can discern how to act in a skillful manner. You can discern whom to spend your time with, what spiritual friends to cultivate, and how to move forward with your goals in a way that is in line with your bodhicitta. It may not be a quick process, and it may be painful at times to always act from your own heart, but it is the surest way to be of benefit to this world and to live a life of empathy and compassion.

9 / BOMBING YOUR WORKPLACE WITH AWAKE

Thus far, we have looked at bodhicitta as a quality we can aspire to cultivate. This is a bit like rousing a motivation to do something. "I want to help all beings." Cool. That is a wonderful intention. However, holding such an intention is only half the battle. It is a bit like saying, "I'm hungry and have arranged to meet this person, so I want to go out to dinner." We're not in the car yet, but we have the intention to go out. We feel like we should. After all, this person is waiting for us.

At a certain point you have to move from aspiring on the Mahayana path to entering it. This is the Buddha's equivalent of "Put your money where your mouth is." Entering the path is actually getting in the car, driving to the restaurant, meeting that person, and eating dinner. That is the difference between the bodhicitta of aspiring and the bodhicitta of entering: instead of just saying, "I'm going to cultivate virtue and an open heart," we actually engage in activity that allows us to do it.

Teachings of this nature are usually offered at a meditation center or yoga studio. They seldom enter the workplace, and often when someone does come into a corporate setting to speak about working with the mind, the focus is practical and not on spirituality. Instead of talking about the various stages of meditation, a consultant might be brought in for "mindfulness-based stress reduction." Something as esoteric-sounding (yet fundamental) as bodhicitta doesn't even get mentioned.

However, the workplace really is *the* place to cultivate bodhicitta. It is where you spend most of your waking hours, so if you do aspire to develop virtue around the clock, you have to actively apply bodhicitta when you are at your desk. Your workplace is where you are faced with discomfort, where frustration rages, where you may at times feel a disconnect between your personal values and those of your employer, and where people are sometimes just jerks. It is the perfect battlefield for unleashing your personal weapon: the bomb of bodhicitta.

As you may recall, the term *bodhi* can be translated as "awake." Think about what it would be like if your entire workplace experienced a hit of awake, even just a few times throughout the day. What if everyone you sat down with paused and experienced their own bodhicitta before speaking or making decisions?

There is a way to make this happen. I am a firm believer that when you offer your own experience of bodhi, you are, in fact, inviting your coworkers to join you in that openhearted space. You are mining the office with a sense of openness. You can let loose your bomb of openness and watch how it radiates out and affects others.

The interesting thing to remember about dropping your bodhi bomb is that you are doing it for the benefit of everyone, not just the people you normally get along with. In traditional meditations on compassion, it is common to contemplate equanimity. It is said that equanimity does not come from sorting a whole mass of people into one pile labeled "friends" and another, larger pile labeled "enemies" and a much, much larger pile labeled "who cares?"

Instead, equanimity means taking a larger view, rising above these petty distinctions, and recognizing that at our core we are all the same. We all possess basic goodness, and we all are striving to be happy. Granted, there are times when some of us are confused about how to achieve that and cause harm for others. Still, the wish for happiness is at the heart of who they are and what they are doing, and we have the option of respecting that intention.

With the perspective of equanimity, we can approach all of our work with a view of nonduality. Compassion doesn't mean thinking of ourselves as more exalted, spiritual, and noble than all our coworkers. In fact, that isn't really compassion at all. That is a form of being obnoxious. Instead, equanimity is the view that no one is different, and so we don't have to divide the world into us versus them; each of us deserves to feel the effects of experiencing bodhicitta.

There are six skillful activities that can unleash the bomb of bodhi, which are known as the six paramitas, or perfections. *Para* can be translated from Sanskrit as "other shore" and *mita* as "arrived." When you have realized your own suffering, you strive to leave the shore of samsara and strike out for the other shore, that of nirvana, or enlightenment.

I think people carry a lot of notions about the term *enlightenment*. Enlightenment does not refer to some holier plain of existence that transcends reality. It is very much reality. It is understanding reality for what it is, in each moment, and how that plays out as suffering when people are unable to see things clearly. So when we say the Buddha attained enlightenment, that does not mean that he went somewhere else and no longer had anything to do with worldly concerns.

In fact, his worldly concerns intensified after he attained enlightenment. All of a sudden he had students looking to him for leadership and a growing organization to attend to. But because of his enlightenment, he was able to see each situation clearly and to lead from his own experience of an awake heart and mind. That is why the Buddha was so successful and is worthy of veneration.

The Buddha taught extensively about the six paramitas,

specifically how they can serve as tools that we can use in cultivating bodhicitta so that we too can move beyond our constant suffering and arrive at the shore of awake. The six paramitas are:

1. *dana* (generosity)
2. *shila* (discipline)
3. *kshanti* (patience)
4. *virya* (exertion)
5. *samadhi* (meditative concentration)
6. *prajna* (wisdom)

These six tools for awakening can be applied to any kind of work, whether you serve as a sales representative, a garbage collector, a nurse, or anything else. They have endured poking and prodding and people practicing them for 2,600 years, so we ought to give them a try.

Generosity

I worked in fund raising for a number of years, and I think anyone who has been in a similar field will agree that it's a very intimate job. Money is a scary topic for a lot of people. Most people feel that they do not have enough of it. Those who do are often worried that others will treat them differently because of it. When you ask someone to donate money to a cause, you are essentially asking them to look deeply at their own neurosis around money and go beyond it, to practice generosity.

Dudjom Rinpoche was an incredibly skilled Buddhist teacher and served as the head of the Nyingma school of Tibetan Buddhism until he passed away in 1987. In his book *A Torch Lighting the Way to Freedom*,[1] he expounds the six paramitas at length. In discussing generosity, he points out that there are three traditional ways to practice generosity.

Giving Material Items

We can give away material possessions. Generosity in this case could be donating clothes to a homeless shelter or letting your friend borrow your car for a cross-country trip or letting a colleague stay in your home. In the workplace, it might mean offering someone a space to work from or connecting someone to research that can help them. In all of these endeavors, we don't offer because we expect anything in return. True generosity is offering without focusing on what you will get out of the exchange, what the other person will do with what you give them, or how the transaction plays out. True generosity is simply offering, without set notions of what should happen next.

Giving Protection from Fear

Sometimes an entire company can become gripped by fear. My friend Dave joined an innovative sustainable energy company approximately a year ago and was promoted within that short period. Due to the state of the economy, the entire company has faced two rounds of layoffs and a 10 percent pay cut for the remaining staff.

In the midst of adjusting to the tension around people losing their jobs and his own personal discomfort with an unexpected pay cut, Dave spoke to me at length about the environmental shift within the company. "It's tense," he said, "and you can't walk into the office without facing a wall of fear." Dave's situation is not unusual. We all have heard similar stories recently. Even spiritual nonprofits I have worked with have had to lay off staff. Even though they tried to be transparent and supportive, it didn't change the fact that people were terrified of losing their jobs and the fear was palpable.

In general, it is hard to offer generosity in an environment infused with a profit-driven mentality. In today's world, it seems even harder given our across-the-board tightening of the belt. In this sort of environment, giving someone protection from fear sounds like an unattainable goal.

In offering protection from fear, while you may not be able to save everyone's job or always protect someone from the office bully or organize everyone's presentations for them so they don't have to worry about failure, you can offer yourself in a supportive manner. You can offer a shoulder to lean on. You can offer a fresh set of eyes on a much-reworked paper. You can take your coworker for a walk to get some fresh air and perspective. You can cover for them so they can deal with personal matters. Or you can simply listen to them vent. In other words, you can offer the gift of your presence generously, without expectation.

GIVING THE GIFT OF DHARMA

There are two aspects to the generosity of giving dharma. The first is that we should give up improper actions—those that we know are harmful to ourselves and others. It could be mindless speech, as discussed earlier, or drowning your workplace frustrations in booze, or making bad meal decisions. That is something of an internal form of generosity, offering up your habitual patterns and negative coping mechanisms and not engaging them anymore. That is giving the gift of dharma to yourself.

The second form of offering the dharma is to offer your experience of it. This is not to say that after reading a few Buddhist books and meditating for a few months, you should proclaim yourself an expert and go preach from a mountaintop. But you can share your experience of how meditation has affected your life and offer your authentic presence in a way that inspires people to try mindfulness out for themselves.

Usually this means showing rather than telling. Instead of bragging about how awesome your meditation is and how everyone at work should try it because they will totally chill out, you can just chill out yourself and see how your presence affects others. Pema Chödrön once said on the topic of generosity, "The main point isn't so much what we give, but that we unlock our habit of clinging."[2] Whether you are giving your material possessions, money, time, service, or presence, it is about offering yourself in a way that unbinds you from your habitual way of relating to the world.

DISCIPLINE

The second paramita is discipline. Discipline often gets a bad rap. People think it's something that is going to be imposed on them, like when you mess up at work and your boss calls you in to his office to discipline you. The Buddhist perspective is much different from that and is based on developing virtue. Dudjom Rinpoche has said that there are three primary ways we can practice discipline.

THE DISCIPLINE OF REFRAINING FROM NEGATIVE ACTIONS

First and foremost, we should aim to refrain from negative activity. This is the discipline of following through on our discernment. If you have been able to discern that you should not hang out with the office gossip and he invites you out for drinks after work, discipline means following through on not hanging out with him. Alternatively, it may mean spending time with him but not engaging in mindless speech.

The more we understand how we engage in negative actions, the easier it becomes to refrain from them. The way we learn about our negative actions is twofold: we meditate and become familiar with our mind, and then we pay attention to our conduct so that if we do make a mistake, we quickly learn from it and vow not to repeat it.

The Discipline of Gathering Positive Actions

Another way to practice discipline is to carry out more positive actions. The more you meditate, the more you turn the tide against the habitual way you have lived your life. One easy way to do this is to determine what "positive actions" means to you.

My personal recommendation is to jot down ten positive actions that you can do at work on any given day. This might be picking up coffee for the security guard in your lobby or agreeing to partner up with a more junior employee who would benefit from your experience and knowledge. It could be complimenting your coworkers on their performance, or grabbing a treat for a friend at the vending machine, or asking about someone's child or ailing relative and making sure they feel heard. When you feel like you are becoming very self-centered and neurotic, pick one of those ten actions and apply the discipline to do it. Practicing discipline in this way means that you are immediately moving beyond thinking about only yourself and instead opening your heart to others.

The Discipline of Working for the Benefit of Sentient Beings

The final form of discipline is based in equanimity. It is the idea that when we refrain from negative actions and cultivate positive ones, we apply the discipline of doing it for everyone. This means that sometimes we must practice a gut-wrenching form of discipline: doing things for people we simply don't like.

In the traditional meditation practices known as loving-kindness contemplations, you begin by extending a sense of kindness and warmth to yourself, then to other people whom you admire or are fond of, to others whom you don't know well, to those whom you have a hard time with, and eventually to all beings. When meditation students practice loving-kindness contemplations, one tricky step is that they have to come up with someone they dislike, an enemy, and offer them a sense of happiness or wish that they will be free from suffering.

I have found that many people have a hard time with this part of the exercise, but not for the reason you may think. Interestingly enough, the hard part seems to be coming up with someone who is a solid "enemy." In today's world, we don't have generations-long feuds that have fueled our hatred since childhood. We don't have the rough equivalent of a Superman / Lex Luthor nemesis relationship.

Adversarial relationships are sparked in much simpler ways today. We have someone who is inconsiderate to us on our morning commute, or writes us terse e-mails, or places blame on us instead of owning up to simple mistakes. These are the people who make us angry and bothered, even if what we feel for them isn't deep hatred.

These are also the people we need to be willing to open our hearts to. Anyone can develop an open heart and offer it to their pet or lover. These beings feel your love all the time and offer it in kind. More often than not, the biggest jerks we know are the ones most in need of kindness and care. So please apply the discipline of working to better their lives too.

PATIENCE

Dudjom Rinpoche has said, "The point of patience is to train so that our altruistic attitude is immovable and irrepressible in the face of those who hurt us with their ingratitude and so forth."[3] Patience is not something that is based in just waiting until you get to do what you want to do, with those people you want to do things with. It is based in relating fully with a situation, even if it annoys the hell out of you.

Patience in Remaining Imperturbable When Wronged

While writing this book, I created an informal survey and asked people what they would like to read about in regard to meditation and how it applies to one's work life. Overwhelmingly, people responded that the major issue they work with is trying to remain mindful when dealing with a boss or coworker who is an asshole and a sloppy communicator.

There is a Chinese proverb that says, "Slander cannot destroy an honest man. . . . when the flood recedes the rock is there." Patience in this sense is simply remaining present when someone is a jerk. When someone wrongs you, you do not need to correct them or lash out at them. This is not a grin-and-bear-it attitude but a matter of allowing enough space into a situation to figure out how to respond in a helpful manner. The good news is that if you remain patient, the water will always recede. Patience, patience, and more patience. That is the antidote to an angry individual. It has a 100 percent success rate.

Patience in Happily Accepting Suffering

The best times to consider patience as an element of our spiritual practice are when we are placed in uncertain or painful situations. I once lost my job because my position was eliminated. I understood the reason I was laid off, but that did not solve my questions about what I should do next or how I would pay my rent.

My first instinct was to do something. Anything, really. Go online and look for job postings, contact every lead I knew, complain about the supreme injustice of it all. However, I realized that the best thing I could do at that moment was offer myself the gift of space. I took some time to practice meditation intensively and waited for clarity to arise within me, rather than trying to find it on a Web site or from friends. Eventually I figured out how to combine my many passions under one umbrella in a way that would be of benefit to others. I needed patience in order to accomplish that. Patience is easy to practice when you know something is going to happen eventually; it is an asset when you don't know what will happen next. If you can smile in the face of uncertainty, you are well trained.

PATIENCE IN ASPIRING TO A TRUE KNOWLEDGE OF REALITY

The final form of patience is based on aspiring to view life as it is. This reinforces the idea of being as present with as much of your life as possible. When you can do that, you have a greater chance of seeing a situation clearly and responding in a way that is in line with what is actually going on rather than your prejudiced notions of how things should be. This is not a simple thing to aspire to, so you have to be patient with yourself as you attempt it.

EXERTION

The fourth paramita is exertion, which encompasses both applying yourself on behalf of others and rousing yourself to think about more than just your own particular situation. Dudjom Rinpoche presents three aspects of exertion.

ARMOR-LIKE EXERTION

We should wear our exertion all the time, constantly remaining vigilant in seeking out opportunities to be of benefit to others. One thing you can do to try out this 24/7 type of exertion is to take a "choose me" approach. Anytime your boss asks for volunteers for an upcoming task, be the first one to throw your hand up in the air. Exert yourself beyond your comfort level. Try this for up to one week and see how you feel at the end of it.

When you don the bodhisattva's armor of exertion, you may find that things that previously felt like a drag all of a sudden have been transformed into opportunities for growth. It feels good to exert yourself beyond your usual laxity.

EXERTION IN APPLICATION

Moving beyond thinking about just *me* doesn't always feel comfortable, so we have to persevere in exerting ourselves to do it. Often we are lost in our own emotional upheavals. When you notice that you are starting to cling tightly to your own comfort, valuing it above the comfort of others, drop the story line of whatever neurotic mess is swirling in your brain and return to the underlying emotion. Acknowledge that emotion, sit with it, but try to cut through the story line around it.

When you have returned to some semblance of calm, take one more step to move beyond thinking solely about yourself. Do one good thing for a coworker and see how that changes your attitude. More often than not, the quickest way to stop feeling lost in your own head is to exert yourself on behalf of another.

EXERTION IN BENEFITING OTHERS

Thus far, exertion seems like it is about just testing our comfort zone. It's more than that. It means that we do not have to view life as a hassle. We can embrace the path of offering ourselves for others as a means to our own happiness. We can put our personal concerns aside to work for something bigger, even if that something bigger is making sure a coworker can take the day off to attend his son's baseball game or staying late so other people won't have to stay late tomorrow. When you exert yourself in this manner, you make others feel good because they are experiencing relief. You feel good because you are living a life that is having an impact on other people. That is true exertion, the type that benefits both ourselves and everyone we encounter.

Meditative Concentration

The fifth paramita, samadhi, has been interpreted in a number of ways. I remember discussing the six paramitas with a group of students and the question arose as to why meditation, which is introduced so early on the Buddhist path, would be fifth on this list of six qualities to cultivate. The simplest answer is that samadhi in this context does not mean simply being with the breath but a true deepening of our meditative experience. It is developing concentration, which can be incredibly useful at work.

Concentration That Produces a Feeling of Well-Being in This Life

The simple fact is that when we are focused and truly mindful, we feel good about what we are doing, whether it is eating a good meal, enjoying a conversation with a client, or completing a successful surgery. In any of these cases, if you bring yourself to the task at hand with concentration, you will feel good about it afterward.

These days, people have an infinite number of distractions available to them. The Internet has made it so that completing a simple report can take ten times longer than it should because your friends want to g-chat with you, your ex has posted pictures of himself on Facebook, and the latest gossip site has just broken a big story. If you spend all your time on distractions like these, you will complete your report eventually, but you'll feel a bit worse for the wear. It may be best to cut down on multitasking and develop a feeling of well-being by bringing yourself entirely to whatever is right in front of you.

Concentration That Gives Rise to Excellent Qualities

The most excellent quality that concentration can give rise to is a sense of awake. If you are able to meditate on whatever is in front of you, you are creating the space for your mind and heart to open to it. Because you are not lost in discursive thoughts, you can see how to apply yourself to the situation fully, from an experience of bodhicitta. From that perspective, you can remain one-pointedly focused on virtue.

CONCENTRATION THAT BENEFITS SENTIENT BEINGS

When you have developed a level of meditative stability, you can be of maximum benefit to everyone you encounter. If you are truly present with people, they begin to feel respected and encouraged. If you bring yourself fully to a project or task, it gets accomplished in a seamless and efficient manner. If you maintain awareness during a difficult conflict, you will be more likely to navigate it effectively. There is no time when deep concentration will not be of benefit to you or others.

PRAJNA

Prajna is often translated from Sanskrit as "wisdom." It is, more specifically, the wisdom to get what the heck is going on in a situation so that you can do something appropriate in that moment. It is not an accumulation of knowledge, or acting in a slow-moving, semicontemplative manner. It is an instant type of wisdom. It is the skill to recognize what needs to be done and to do it.

A longer definition of prajna, offered by Dudjom Rinpoche, is "intelligence that perfectly discerns the nature of all phenomena." It is wisdom that is in tune with what is. It is intelligence that is perceptive and clear. There are three main ways to let this form of intelligence guide your activity.

THE WISDOM OF LISTENING

Listening is a lost art in our society. There is great wisdom in taking the time to hear someone out and give yourself the space to understand what they are trying to communicate. When you sit down to meet with someone, you can take the attitude of not needing to come up with an immediate solution to whatever the issue is. You can avoid interrupting them or making assumptions and instead listen deeply.

Similarly, in developing prajna, you can't just walk into a meeting and tell everyone about all your great ideas. First, you have to listen deeply to everyone you encounter. The more questions you ask, the more you can see a situation for what it is. The more you listen, the more you will eventually be able to express yourself clearly to others.

THE WISDOM OF REFLECTING/CONTEMPLATING

After deeply listening to a variety of opinions, you should chew on them. See what truth sits with you and what does not. Reflect on what has been offered to you. There is an element of patience in this process as you continue to contemplate what you have heard, sorting through what comments ring true and which you think ought to be disregarded. Instead of jumping into the habitual thing we all do, which is trying to present a solution or fix something, allow yourself time for wisdom to arise.

THE WISDOM OF MEDITATING

Finally, allow your contemplations to sink in as an act of meditation. The discursive thoughts that came up will naturally dissipate. What truths have come to you will remain. Sitting with the reality of the situation, you develop certainty in those facts. You can realize those truths in your life and work. Then you are prepared to act.

Interestingly enough, though prajna is the final paramita, it is the most important one. It is the ability to see a situation clearly, without layering it with your own expectations or opinions. Having dropped that baggage at the door, you can see what's best for everyone, as opposed to what's comfortable for you.

It is said that when we develop the perspective of prajna, all of the other paramitas are made perfect. It is the essential element that lights the fuse on the bomb of bodhi.

Sakyong Mipham Rinpoche wrote, "When our attitude is open, we can have fun with what the world presents."[4] The workplace does not have to be a battleground; that is just one way to view it. Instead we can view it as a fun factory. You can begin by offering the paramitas to yourself, seeing how they influence your behavior. See if they perk you up, if you feel uplifted and joyful because of them. See if you become more efficient at your work. Then you can begin offering the paramitas to others, both the individuals you like and those you have a hard time with. Eventually, you can offer this perfect activity to everyone you meet. If you are able to offer your heart in this way, it can transform not just your workplace but the entire world.

10 / KARMA, THE SIX REALMS, AND WHY YOU SHOULD STOP BEING A JERK

Karma is often misunderstood in the West. Sometimes people confuse karma with fate. "It must be my karma that I got fired," they cry out, resigning themselves to the unfortunate scenario.

I once was contacted by a writer for popular television shows. He was pitching an idea for a new series featuring a female detective who had been raised in monasteries and was successful at solving crimes because of her deep Buddhist insight. He would pitch me different scenes and ask how a "typical" Buddhist might react differently from a non-Buddhist cop.

It was fun at the time, but at one point he described a scene where a drug dealer had been shot down. He asked if it was appropriate to say, "Well, he got what was coming to him; that's his karma." After years of seeing karma misrepresented in television and movies, I gave him a polite earful on the Buddhist concept of cause and effect and how it plays out over lifetimes. "Huh?" he said. "I don't think I can include all of that in the script." Because karma is so complex, it is no wonder it is misrepresented in popular culture.

The popular understanding of karma is that action and result have a one-to-one correlation; for example, if you do something bad like sell someone drugs, then you will ultimately get shot. That's a very simple way to think of it, and although it's not entirely wrong, it's not entirely right either.

From a Buddhist point of view, karma is the law of cause and effect, which plays out over multiple lifetimes. Instead of saying a drug dealer got shot because he sold drugs, a meditation teacher might say that he more likely was shot because, to pick a random example, several lifetimes prior he might have been a panda bear who violently killed a neighbor panda bear who threatened him. These multiple lifetimes are not based on an everlasting soul or being but on what is known in Tibetan as *kunshi nampar shepa* or in Sanskrit as the *alaya* (abode) consciousness.

Think of the alaya consciousness as a giant warehouse. It is white and pristine. This is representative of our basic state. This giant warehouse exists to house your virtuous and unvirtuous actions, known respectively in Tibetan as *gewa* and *migewa*. If you engage in positive actions, such as helping a coworker out of a jam, then it is like walking into the alaya warehouse with rose water on your feet. This sort of activity creates the cause for a future rebirth in which you can enjoy your life and be of benefit to others. If you screw your coworker over, though, it is like walking into the warehouse with muddy shoes on. Your negative actions will be imprinted on your alaya consciousness like mud on a white carpet.

Your alaya, which is basically clear and neutral, gets imprinted with your virtuous and unvirtuous activity. It holds the imprints of positive and negative actions that will, in some way, give rise to results in this or another lifetime. This is different from the one-to-one correlation that is often assumed in discussions about karma, so it is worth considering our own experience to try to determine what this karmic warehouse means for us.

The Buddha said that we have to test the truth of his teachings. He encouraged us to check whether anything he taught meshes with our own experience. He emphasized this idea to the extent that he said that if we don't have an actual experience of something he taught, we should not take it at face value.

I don't know about you, but the idea of rebirth has always been a hard one for me to wrap my mind around. I have heard stories of parents claiming their young child would talk at length about a previous life, and I have read accounts of individuals who are known in Tibet as *delogs*, people who have supposedly died and then come back to life with tales about the various experiences they had. Personally, I have no recollection of my own past lives or deaths.

As such, I have a hard time fully developing faith in this Buddhist concept. This is not to denigrate this traditional idea, but I do encourage you to consider your own experience of death and rebirth and come to your own conclusion on this set of teachings.

Even though I can't remember previous lifetimes, I have experienced that what you do in this life lays the ground for the future. I am open to the idea that you could be laying the ground for a future rebirth, but I believe you could also be laying the ground for situations you will deal with in this life.

After all, the cycle of suffering we find ourselves in, samsara, is based in our own mind. It is reinforced every time we solidify a negative habitual pattern. If you continuously give in to jealousy over your friends' career success, then you are planting seeds for more jealousy in this very lifetime. You are making it easier to become attached to that root emotion. However, if you take delight in others' success, then you are planting seeds that destroy envy.

In *Turning the Mind into an Ally*, Sakyong Mipham Rinpoche writes, "If we plant peaches, we're always going to get peaches. If we plant pears, we're always going to get pears."[1] This is perhaps the simplest and clearest description of karma I have ever read. Whatever seeds you plant in your own mind will bear fruit appropriately. That is why we should abandon negative deeds, devote our time to virtuous actions, and every day take the time to examine ourselves to make sure we're planting the seeds for a good life that is helpful to others.

The Six Realms

According to the Buddhist canon, there are six realms of existence, although you might not have any memory of actual lifetimes spent in some of them. It may be helpful to think of them as psychological states, which is how they are often introduced. Whether we think of them as places we go to when we die or states of mind we experience in this lifetime, we can examine ourselves and see how we create the causes for encountering these six realms.

The Hell Realm

It is said that even one moment of anger can be like immersing your body in a swamp and running muddy into your alaya warehouse and rolling around; you are dooming yourself to the hell realm. The hell realms are said to be places of various kinds of torment. There are hot hell realms, where you are burned in various ways, as well as cold hell realms, where you freeze in various ways. There are hells where you are poked and prodded and eaten in myriad ways, but you keep coming back to your whole body and repeating the torment.

Psychologically speaking, we have all been in this realm. You may have experienced the hot hell realms when your superior did something disrespectful and you became furious. You may have experienced the cold hell realms when you made a mistake and your coworkers responded by shooting you icy glares and being terse in your presence. You may have entered into a habitual relationship with someone at work in which you constantly feel like he is poking and prodding at everything you do, waiting to ambush you and get you written up by your boss.

The point here is that when you experience anger, you don't have to act on it and give in to perpetuating negative actions. You can feel the hot and the cold, the poking and prodding, without lashing out and creating harm for yourself and others. Experiencing these strong emotional states but not giving in to them is how we sow the seeds of virtue.

THE HUNGRY-GHOST REALM

The hungry-ghost realm is based in jealousy and stinginess. It is said that when you are born into this realm, you take on the form of a hungry ghost, a being who suffers from extreme hunger and thirst. Hungry ghosts are said to have mouths the size of a needle's eye and stomachs the size of mountains. Their necks are so thin that they cannot pass any food down to the stomach, so while the hungry ghost is starving, it cannot eat and is lost in a state of yearning for an entire lifetime.

While you may not have recent memories of living the life of such a being, the idea of yearning is probably not far from your experience. We constantly long to fulfill our physical desires but are never satisfied with what we get. If a hungry ghost does manage to get food down its throat, it is only reminded of what it has been missing, and its desire for more increases exponentially.

This hungry-ghost lifestyle might manifest as trying to hoard what you do have, neglecting the joy that generosity brings, and living like a pack rat. Or you might spend all your time wishing for job opportunities that you don't have instead of appreciating your current situation. When you engage in this mentality, you are lost in desire and do not experience joy. By cutting through stinginess and craving, you can experience your life more fully and are planting the seeds for more positive things to occur in your life (or lifetimes).

THE ANIMAL REALM

Finally, a realm that we know for sure exists. I have often heard people look at their cat and joke, "In my next lifetime, I want to come back as a cat. My cat doesn't have to do anything but eat and sleep and play." The thing about the animal realm, though, is that it is not all fun and games.

Even your cat suffers from a lack of freedom. You and I can go for a bike ride, go out with friends, or choose how we spend our free time. Your cat is basically stuck at home or, if she gets adventurous, in the immediate area. She cannot feed herself; she relies on humans for food and will be hungry until someone feeds her. So in some sense, cats live a very dependent life.

And yet a cat's existence is a pretty good lifestyle for the animal realm. Most animals live in the wild and experience the constant fear of being attacked or eaten. They can never truly relax, because they either need to hunt for food or are being hunted themselves.

Last but not least, it is said that the animal realm is not a good one to be born into because of animals' limited intelligence. They are unable to meditate and become familiar with their own mind, and thus are constantly yanked around by instinctual urges. They suffer from bewilderment and have no hope of distinguishing between virtue and nonvirtue.

From a psychological point of view, this idea of bewilderment may not seem too far off. Perhaps you butt heads with various people at work and repeatedly end up in the same cyclical arguments with them. Now, if you become familiar with your own mind through the practice of meditation, you are less likely to hunt and be hunted in this way. You can step away from bewilderment and live a life of virtue.

THE HUMAN REALM

The human realm is said to be the best possible birth, because we have the ability to work with our mind and become a better person. This is the sole realm in which we can seek awakening.

At the same time, the human realm is marked by its own pains. We suffer from the pains of birth, aging, sickness, and death. While we may be smarter than, say, certain animals, that intelligence often plays out in our desperately seeking pleasure and avoiding pain. We become lost in desire. The nice thing about the human realm is that we can snap out of the cycle of suffering we find ourselves in.

Because we have this opportunity, we need to take advantage of it. There is a traditional metaphor that illustrates how rare it is to be born into the human realm. Imagine that the whole world was an ocean, and on its surface, a wooden yoke. For those of you who aren't familiar with this term, a yoke is a wooden structure that goes around the neck of an ox. This yoke floats across the sea in all directions. Underneath the surface of the ocean is a blind tortoise that lives for many thousands of years but only comes up to poke his head through the surface once every century. It is said that it is more likely for that tortoise to poke through the hole of the yoke floating somewhere on the ocean than it is for someone to obtain a precious human birth. Thus, it is a rare and precious opportunity.

Lately a term has become quite popular because of rappers like Drake and Lil Wayne: YOLO (you only live once). In other words, make the most of your life. Whether you believe in rebirth or not, you can examine your life and see if you are making the most of it. You can contemplate whether you are wasting your life in distraction or pursuing virtuous activity, bettering yourself and others.

THE JEALOUS-GOD REALM

The jealous-god realm is said to be inhabited by demigods. They live long lives that are wasted in jealousy of gods who have more than they do. As a result, they constantly try to wage war against the higher gods but are easily defeated.

A rough equivalent of this jealous-god scenario may play out when your colleagues are promoted ahead of you. They receive more money and more praise, they're dressing better, and you envy them their success. You feel that you should have received all of these perks so you act out your jealousy and try to tear them down through gossip and slander. However, because they were promoted based on their own merits, your envious acts don't really hurt them but only make you look bad. Thus, it is better to learn to sit with your jealousy and let it pass like a cloud moving across the sky instead of engaging in unvirtuous activity.

THE GOD REALM

The sixth realm is the god realm. Gods are not eternal in the Buddhist tradition, but they do have an extended lifetime of many years. This is the reward for having engaged in virtue and accumulated a large amount of positive karma. For the majority of their lifetime the gods are youthful and healthy. They live a life without discord and enjoy every aspect of their day-to-day existence. If they suffer during this portion of their lives, it is from pride in how good they have it.

However, at some point they begin to die. Their looks fade and they begin to smell. Their friends all avoid them and they are left to their own devices to deal with this first real burst of suffering they are experiencing. Because their lives are so long, this period lasts for generations and is absolutely unbearable. It is said this gradual decline is actually the most painful experience of all of the various realms of samsara.

When I go to visit my sister in Beverly Hills, I often experience that neighborhood as a god realm. Some people there put a great deal of effort into their looks, maintaining their fame, and making sure they have more money than their neighbors. There is a lot of pride in that lifestyle. However, as soon as someone's movie flops or they make a large public gaffe, people start to shun them. They find themselves friendless and without money, and they can no longer maintain their good looks. This incredible loss must be very painful.

Even if we do not have tremendous money and fame, we all have fallen victim to the feeling that an external factor, be it a relationship, a job, or friends, would bring us everlasting happiness. Since we cannot avoid impermanence, we must realize that things change and we will suffer this form of loss. Knowing that things change is part of our path; it allows us to appreciate them more. We loosen our attachment when we realize the nature of impermanence, and we are then more likely to be generous and engage in other virtuous activity.

The six realms are based in the same three root emotions, aggression, passion, and ignorance, discussed earlier. We become lost in the hell realm when we fall victim to anger and aggression. We wander in the hungry-ghost realm when we are stingy and passionately desirous of things we cannot have. We meander in the animal realm when we are lost in ignorance. The human realm is marked by the desire for pleasure and the desire to avoid pain. The jealous-god realm is based in aggression, specifically the aggression of acting out against beings that we perceive as having more than we do. The god realm is a place of ignorance, where we do not realize the nature of change.

When we examine the six realms, we can see that, while they may or may not be actual places where we are reborn, they are definitely states of mind we all lose ourselves in. Understanding the realms encourages us to pursue virtuous activity and avoid negative behavior. In order to do that, we need to examine ourselves constantly.

The more you examine yourself, the more you will see how you wander into these various realms through the simplest of actions. As Sakyong Mipham Rinpoche has said about karma, "One word too many, and our friend blows his lid. Two little words, and we've married somebody. We never know at exactly what moment one action or word is going to trigger another, but everything we do sets something else in motion."[2]

When you examine yourself with karma in mind, you will live a life that you can be proud of, that can lead to a good rebirth (if you believe in reincarnation), and that will bring about great heaps of virtue.

EXERCISE FOR NOT BEING A JERK AT WORK
(AND DEVELOPING GOOD KARMA)

When we meditate on the breath, we come back to it over and over again. Coming back to the breath cuts through habitual patterns and thoughts. Another way to meditate is on a phrase or question. You can take a particular Buddhist concept, like karma or compassion, and meditate on it in order to bring it more fully into your experience off the meditation cushion.

One such concept worth contemplating is the notion that all beings have been your mother. It is said that we have lived so many lifetimes that all beings have been connected with one another at different points. So, even someone who cuts you off during your morning commute or someone who continually puts you down was, in some past lifetime, your mother, who bore you and cared for you. They could have been a mother ant when you were a child ant, but the same principle applies. Even if you have issues with your current mother, you cannot argue that without her you would not have this precious life.

Begin this contemplation by practicing shamatha meditation for at least ten minutes. Once you have grounded yourself in the physical experience of your breathing, you can turn your mind to the formal contemplation.

Start by considering the kindness of your own mother. Sit with her image and see what qualities or memories come up. It may be helpful to sit with the phrase *I give thanks for her kindness.* You may see some resentment or conflicting feelings arise. That is okay. But see if you can get to the point where you recall very kind things that your mother has done or sacrifices she made to ensure your well-being.

Then bring to mind the name or image of someone you love dearly—a partner, a friend, or a person you admire a great deal. Bring your attention to the phrase *This being has been my mother*. Feel free to insert the person's name instead of "this being." Consider the incredible generosity this person may have offered to you. If it is more helpful, you can instead use the phrase *I give thanks for their kindness*.

Having started with your own mother and moved on to another individual you love, you can take two minutes and contemplate the same phrases about a friend, someone who is generally supportive of you or is always there for you in a time of need. You know their kindness already, so turn your mind to the idea that they may have shown you even more kindness in a past life.

After two minutes on that individual, bring to mind someone you don't know as well and neither dislike nor like all that much; they just sort of exist in the background of your life. It could be someone who works down the hall from you, or your regular barista. Even if you don't know their name, consider that *This being has been my mother. I give thanks for their kindness*. They have shown you great care and support in the past.

Next bring to mind someone whom you don't get along with. This is the "enemy" step mentioned before. If you don't have someone you regularly have a beef with, just think of someone who annoyed you on your commute or who gets on your nerves from time to time. Even if strong emotions rear their head, bring your mind to the phrase *This being has been my mother* or *I give thanks for their kindness*. If nothing else, you can feel gratitude that their rudeness gives you something with which to practice compassion; that is a form of kindness in itself.

After spending a few minutes contemplating this difficult person, think of these five individuals together. Holding each of their images in mind, dissolve the boundaries of opinion around them and collectively consider them with the same appreciation you would your mother.

A minute or two later, extend your feeling of gratitude further. Without discrimination, offer your sense of appreciation to people in your home or workplace, then your city, your state, and farther out, recognizing that all of these beings have, at one point, been your mother.

Then rest. Drop the formal contemplation and just be present with whatever emotion has arisen. You might feel like you have just given thanks, or a larger sense of empathy. Whatever feeling has come up, rest with that. Rest your mind in that state.

The more we engage in this type of contemplation, the more we develop a sense of equanimity and the more we are able to relate to all sorts of people with compassion and empathy. If we consider everyone we encounter as someone who has previously shown us kindness, we are less likely to be a jerk and more willing to love unconditionally, in the office and throughout our day.

11 / THREE STEPS FOR CREATING SOCIAL CHANGE THROUGH INNER CHANGE

I believe that thoughtful young people entering the job force today are not just interested in making lots of money; they want to be of benefit to the world too. They want to make other people's lives better in addition to their own. A recent study developed by the Career Advisory Board showed that one of the most important factors for the millennial generation when looking for a job was that they felt the work they are doing is meaningful. The notion of doing something meaningful outranked "high pay" and "sense of accomplishment."[1]

What meaningful work looks like in today's world can be confusing, but I believe that if you hold the view of compassion, understand cause and effect, and want to apply the six paramitas, you can be the very change you want to see in the world and effect that change in the culture around you.

The first week I arrived at college, the twin towers fell. I remember getting up that morning, walking into my dorm's common room, and seeing the footage on TV. My first instinct was a good one: I returned to my room and engaged in compassion meditation practices, offering my heart and sympathy to all those affected by this tragedy.

After that initial wave of heartbreak passed, I became outraged. It was only a few weeks later that I, along with three hundred others, took to the streets of Hartford, Connecticut. We were protesting what we perceived as the knee-jerk reaction of the U.S. government in bombing Afghanistan. In my mind, the swift and deadly response to the September 11 attacks was unjust and was likely to hurt more innocents than terrorists, further fueling the fires of aggression that have engulfed our world.

I was just one guy lost in a wave of anger and frustration, overwhelmed by the emotions of those chanting and bustling around me. Meanwhile, police officers began to set up roadblocks and attempted to break up the protest. Their rage over the 9/11 attacks fueled our own, and before too long the protest erupted into violence.

From there I only have fragmented images. A police officer daring me to step off the sidewalk and embrace arrest. A sixty-year-old man being struck, falling to the ground, and wailing, "I can't see! I think they broke my ribs!" Police officers hovering menacingly over him. A look of pure hatred on the face of one officer as he held up a can of pepper spray. A crowd in the lobby of an office building unwilling to let me wash the burn from my eyes and neck. A group of dejected protesters handcuffed together in the back of a paddy wagon. A processing officer telling me that I wouldn't make it through the weekend in jail—that I would be beaten to death by my own shoes.

I spent forty-eight hours in jail, and during that time I began to reflect on how I ended up surrounded by murderers and drug dealers, facing criminal charges, a part of the first major post-9/11 protest arrest. One conclusion I came to is that I do not regret moving to aid that older gentleman. He was hurt and my instinct was to help. I cannot fault that instinct, nor would I want to change it.

At the same time, I could not help feeling that my years of meditation training had gone out the window that day. International violence had begotten international violence, striking the

United States a crushing blow. My initial instinct to touch base with my own sadness was eventually clouded over in the midst of a nationwide atmosphere of anger and terror. I had become lost in the post-9/11 fog. I had become the problem, as opposed to the solution, by letting my rage fuel my actions in the midst of a protest. I did not represent the peace I wanted to see in the world that day, only the fear and chaos that was engulfing it.

When strong emotions like anger and fear arise on the meditation cushion, we know instinctively that we ought to cut through them gently yet decisively. It could be feeling that a coworker is treating you unfairly, that you are anxious about a friend's health, or that you are reliving an angry conversation that happened hours ago.

Regardless of the story line, the point of our meditation practice is to recognize the underlying emotions and, before getting caught up in them, to see them as impermanent. You can see the story lines as something other than what is currently going on in your present experience. From there you can return to the breath. This is our practice on and off the meditation cushion.

Yet, over a dozen years ago, when faced with a surging crowd of protesters and an equally charged crowd of officers of the law, I caved in. I bought in to the generations-old story line of us versus them. I gave in to the belief that we were in the right, which meant the police must have been in the wrong. I stopped listening to my own basic goodness, to my understanding of karma, and to my impulse to respect the six paramitas. Instead I gave in to the same sense of dualism that snowballs into violence and destruction—the same enraged, polarized notions that created the 9/11 tragedy in the first place.

Throughout the following year, as I attended court dates and met with my parole officer, I had time to reflect on my mistake and how Generation O has a real opportunity to do something radical and, in my opinion, more productive to create social change.

I won't knock anyone who wants to peacefully protest. At the same time, the poster person for peaceful protest, Mahatma Gandhi, once said that we should strive to be the change we want to see in the world. That day in Hartford, no one represented peaceful change. International protests today seem to betray the same feelings of dualistic aggression as the Hartford protest years ago.

An angry protester demanding peace seems paradoxical. To quote the comedian George Carlin, "Fighting for peace is like screwing for virginity." It simply doesn't make sense. So what can young people in the West do to make our voices heard in a skillful and compassionate manner? How can we create change through embodying our ideals? And how can this manifest as we engage our work over the decades to come?

STEP 1: CUTTING THROUGH FIXED VIEWS

The first step is to learn to work with our expectations. We all have them: The idea for what the world would be like if only X, Y, and Z would change. The utopia we know we could achieve if only the right people were elected, the right economic checks were put in place, the right sorts of companies were given a chance to succeed. The problem with these fixed views is that they are the basis for dualistic thinking. If you go into the world with the notion that your opinions are better than everyone else's and try to force them down people's throats, you are only propagating aggression.

In 2012 I worked for Barack Obama's reelection campaign in the swing state of Ohio. Because President Obama had a background in community organizing, the model for his campaign reflected the values he had developed during that time. He sent us, his staff, into neighborhoods to talk with people—but not to inform them why he was the best candidate or what they ought to do to support him. Instead, he asked us to have genuine conversations with people. To find out what issues they cared about.

To determine what mattered to them. To connect with them without forcing our own point of view on anyone.

When I trained volunteers for campaign work, I would point out that we could offer undecided voters lots of statistical information. We could talk to them about the thirty-one consecutive months of job growth during the president's first term or his risky bailout of the auto industry that saved so many jobs in Ohio and elsewhere. But I asked them instead to do what was asked of me: to share their personal stories about why they wanted to support the president and listen deeply to whatever the person had to say.

I remember visiting the home of Iras, a seventy-eight-year-old woman whose mobility was limited to her home due to a wide variety of ailments. She lived on Social Security in a small apartment on the west side of Columbus, Ohio. My job, in this case, was not to lecture Iras about why she should volunteer for the Obama campaign. I simply sat down and listened to her story. It turned out that she was terrified about the health care changes proposed by Mitt Romney.

"I don't need much," Iras said. "I have my couch. I have my television. I used to have a dining room table, but I sold it to make room for my oxygen tank. I deserve this much. I worked for this much." I agreed. "Romney doesn't know what it's like for people like me. Obama knows people. He is in touch with lower-income people. If Romney is elected," she said, "Social Security will be in jeopardy. I might as well take out my oxygen and go into the corner and die. If he's elected, I can't afford to live."

Iras offered this point of view as a matter of fact. She was not trying to be melodramatic. If I had tried to dissuade her from this point of view, I realized I would be doing her a disservice. Iras volunteered to call undecided voters and share her story. I knew I could trust her to make these sorts of phone calls, because she was not trying to force her view on anyone. She was simply able to be present and share her heart. That allowed me (and others) to really want to listen to her, and she was actually a great listener herself.

When you find that you have been trying to push your personal trip on someone at work, you can meditate and examine where these fixed views come from. You can sit on the cushion, breath after breath, and watch the display of your mind. As thoughts come and go, it's almost like you're watching a really funny, scary, and sometimes obnoxious movie play out right before your eyes. Yet you can just watch this display, gently coming back to the breath over and over again.

At a certain point, you may see certain themes come up repeatedly. This is when you can begin to discern how you get hooked by fixed views. You might even develop a sense of humor about it. In some sense, it's absurd that you can be sitting in your apartment yet your mind will be in your office, rehashing a confrontation with a colleague, perpetuating that idea that you're right and they are wrong. That confrontation happened days ago!

To overcome this type of habitual pattern, you can gently return to something that is unwaveringly true: the present moment. On the Obama campaign, it was drilled into our heads that every minute, every conversation, was essential to whether the president would get reelected. That meant that we had to be fully there for every moment of every workday. Adopting this view was excellent training and something we could all strive to engage regardless of work. By continuously coming back to the present, we are learning to free ourselves from fixed points of view. That is an important first step in creating change, at work and in society.

STEP 2: RAISING YOUR GAZE

As you get to know your mind, you see where you get hooked by fixed emotions, but they no longer get their hooks into you like they used to. You come to recognize when you stray into one of the six realms. Then you start to recognize people around you similarly lost in the fog of their own emotional states. As you are freed from just listening to and expounding upon your own fixed views, you become more available to notice the emotional turmoil of those around you.

Perhaps you used to be dragged down by strong emotions. Perhaps it felt like you were lost in a waterfall of passion, aggression, and bewilderment. However, because of serious hours logged on the meditation cushion, that waterfall seems less powerful—now it is more like a stream. You're not hopping off the cushion fully enlightened, but you have a greater familiarity with your own habitual patterns and are moving toward opening your heart more fully to others, unconditionally.

From the recognition that everyone around us experiences the same things we do, compassion naturally dawns. You feel a tug at your heart and you want to help people out from under their own personal waterfalls of disturbing emotions.

In his article "Innovation Starts with Empathy," Dev Patnaik points out that the quickest and most effective way for a company to prosper is for its leaders to develop empathy for the world around them. He tells the story of a team from a luxury automobile company that went to San Francisco in the hope of figuring out why they were not attracting new, young customers.[2]

Instead of running through graphs and data, Dev and his colleagues met with members of the company's target demographic and ran through exercises in which they had to get to know one another. The final test was that each team, having spent a little time with a young Californian, was given $50 to go out and buy that person a gift. One team came back with touristy San Francisco gifts, which revealed that they had not really seen and understood their native friend. Giving a San Franciscan an "I Heart SF" T-shirt showed that they didn't connect with their target audience or understand what they would want or need, automobile-wise or otherwise.

But another team did prove that they could connect with their target audience. They came back with more thoughtful gifts: to an aspiring entrepreneur they gave a book on building out your company, with a tiny amount of seed money tucked into the front cover. This team from the luxury car company had taken the time to put themselves in the shoes of their young target audience and come to understand their priorities and goals, and thus they would be more successful in connecting with and targeting them in the long run.

This charming story makes Dev's point clear: the more we can empathize with coworkers, clients, and even superiors, the better we will be able to understand them. Having understood them and seen them for who they are, we will be able to figure out how best to engage in compassionate activity and create change based on what needs to happen, as opposed to our ideas about what needs to happen.

To return to Obama's campaign, it became clear to me that while his opponent spent money on robo-calls and expensive ads, the president had trusted genuine human interactions to get his campaign message out. He asked his staff nationwide to meet with people one-on-one in their homes and neighborhoods and to speak and listen from the heart so that authentic communication occurred. Many of us stationed in lower-income neighborhoods experienced wave after wave of empathy for people who were struggling. Even after the campaign, many of us are in touch with volunteers we encountered and are working to continue to aid in empowering them as leaders in their neighborhoods and their lives.

STEP 3: COMPASSIONATE ACTIVITY

Having raised our gaze, we can take our experience of empathy and recommit to a strong motivation: we want to be of benefit. We can have faith that it's possible to be of benefit, because we are no longer so attached to our own fixed expectations. This is the experience of prajna, the wisdom that sees situations clearly and allows us to exercise the six paramitas accordingly.

Instead of trying to yell our ideas for societal change into

existence, we have the opportunity to infiltrate the same organizations we seek to transform and create the change from
within. If you work as a cashier, you can engage the hundreds
of customers you see each day with an open heart and a desire
to be helpful. If you work in a hospital, you can be present with
everyone you encounter—patients as well as their families—
and extend a caring presence to them. If you work in sales, you
can listen deeply to your customers and make sure they feel
like their needs are heard and met. We can maintain an open
heart, even in tough corporate settings, and let our compassion
touch others.

As upsets occur, we can develop faith that the power of an
open heart can accommodate even the hardest situations. In
Hagakure it is said, "When meeting calamities or difficult situations, it is not enough to simply say that one is not at all flus-
tered. When meeting difficult situations, one should dash
forward bravely and with joy."[3] This is going beyond just avoiding the upsetting aspects of your work or life; we must rush
bravely into the storm. If you confront tough situations in this
manner, you will experience joy in this precious opportunity
we have to offer our hearts.

I realize that, like many aspects of the Buddhist path, this
one is easier said than done. However, the alternative is bleak.
You could live outside "the system" and only hang out with
people who share your ideals. I don't think that many of us intend to create that sort of fringe or cult society. Instead, I think
most people today want to change the world they grew up in
and improve their work environment.

I believe that there are thousands, if not millions, of people
out there who want to live their lives in accordance with their
own bodhicitta. They want to start a business based on compassionate activity, or run a team within their company dedicated
to mindfully listening to and encouraging one another, or create art that will inspire others to be kinder people. They want to
bring the qualities they want to cultivate into jobs where they
are not usually found and see how that helps others. I believe

we are a generation that wants to create positive change, but we have not yet woken up to our potential to do so.

I think that through embodying the compassion we so often strive to practice, including deepening our understanding of karma and the six paramitas, we can realize that potential. We can become known as kind and trusted leaders. People at school, at work, or even in our own families will naturally pick up on our positive energy. They will be inspired, and, in the face of compassion, often they will adapt their behavior to be more accepting and open as well.

If we can continuously connect to the power of our own open heart, I believe we can indeed create societal change over time. We can use our work situation as a jumping-off point for sharing our heart more widely with everyone we encounter. We can reflect each day on whether what we have done has helped others or created positive change in the world. Through this gradual process, we can build a society that is based in empathy and compassion.

In this way, societal change might not look like what we thought it would, but we still shape the world around us in a positive and healthy way. At the end of the day, it's not someone else who will change your work environment or even our society for the better. It's you. It's always been you and will always be you. So let's all please step up and help this world progress further toward compassion and empathy. It's not up to some elusive "them"—it's up to us.

12 / FIVE SLOGANS FOR EMPATHY AND COMPASSION

Every day, you have an impact on others in either a positive or a negative way. It is up to you to decide if you want to overcome whatever sense of apathy you may feel today and rouse yourself to engage in virtuous activity, or if you prefer to sink into lazy self-centeredness.

You have the choice, in any given moment, to wake up to bodhicitta. In part 1, we looked at the Hinayana view of how we can work with our own mind to be present and conscious in our work. Here we are exploring the Mahayana view of expanding that process so we can drop fixed expectations and be available to everyone we encounter, regardless of what our employment is. If you can move beyond thinking only about yourself and open up to an empathetic point of view, then you will be able to come home from work and feel good about the life you are living.

At the end of part 1, we began exploring the Mahayana teachings of Atisha on lojong, or mind training. We can continue our examination of the lojong teachings, looking at how they relate to discerning virtuous activity and practicing compassion through the six paramitas. The following five slogans seem particularly relevant to keeping an open heart at work.

When the world is filled with evil, transform all mishaps into the path of bodhi.

This might be the most challenging instruction Atisha has to offer us. He is saying that it is easy to keep an open heart when we are surrounded by puppies and loving friends and family. When we are confronted with bona fide evil, particularly in the workplace, it is difficult to maintain a sense of bodhi.

Even though you may desire to cultivate the qualities you want to see in the world, you may not be in the best work environment for doing so. Often we are forced to work in less than ideal positions. We may not always even agree with our company's mission. We may feel like we are supporting a corporate behemoth when we really want to be putting food in the mouths of small children. While it is helpful to continue to evaluate your intention and determine if your livelihood suits you, it might be even more helpful to consider Atisha's advice. When in the belly of the beast, you can create tremendous positive change simply by taking whatever comes up at work as an opportunity to exhibit the power of an open heart.

Imagine crawling into a dark cave. It's claustrophobic and stuffy, and you really don't want to be there. But suddenly you remember that you have a flashlight in your pocket. Turning that flashlight on, even for a moment, greatly changes the environment. You can see it clearly for what it is and don't need to be so intimidated by it. You can see how to manage the cave in a skillful and direct manner, instead of flailing around mindlessly. That cave is an evil-filled workplace. The flashlight is your bodhicitta. The beauty of bodhicitta is that you never will run out of batteries; it is always available.

Whatever you meet unexpectedly, join with meditation.

A wide variety of things come up unexpectedly in the workplace. Some of them leave us feeling groundless, as if the rug has been pulled out from under us. All kinds of scary things seem to be happening in today's rough economy—layoffs, pay cuts, and so on. On the other hand, unexpected positive things can come your way too—you might be contacted by a head hunter or offered a significant bonus for a job well done. In both these scenarios, you should join what happens with the mind of meditation.

Chögyam Trungpa Rinpoche has commented that *join* is an important word here—it is like bringing together bread and butter. When you bring together unexpected events and meditation, it similarly creates a complete scenario. There is an innocent quality here, where we allow our meditation just to be available to accommodate whatever might arise, whether it is good or bad, for us or against us. We don't discriminate. It is all fodder for our journey. As Trungpa Rinpoche has said, "Whatever shakes you should without delay, right away, be incorporated into the path."[1]

To further the discussion of karma and the alaya, when you are thrown a curveball in life, you are immediately offered two doors that you can walk through. Both open into your warehouse consciousness. One door is marked MEDITATION AND VIRTUOUS ACTIVITY and the other PASSION AGGRESSION IGNORANCE DANGER KEEP OUT. Perhaps it is all those capital letters, but we often miss the meditation door and run straight toward this doorway of habitual patterns. Throwing ourselves through that door, we fall into a puddle of mud and limp into negative activity and consequences. There is a large puddle of mud right before it. We fall in and we stumble into the alaya with dirt flying everywhere.

If we train ourselves to slow down enough to see the MEDITATION AND VIRTUOUS ACTIVITY door, we can engage our surprise situation with ease and kindness, walking lightly through rose water as we proceed to propagate virtue. Both doors exist; it is up to you which one you want to enter when faced with unexpected situations.

Don't act with a twist.

Short and sweet, this lojong slogan encourages you to be straightforward in all your workplace interactions as well as your meditation practice. If you decide to be a Goody Two-shoes because you think that will help you get ahead at work, you won't be genuine. Similarly, if you think of compassion as some intellectual pursuit that will benefit you in the long run, that is also a fallacious view.

The idea that you should do something good simply because you will benefit from it is a twist. Instead, you should exercise compassion and empathy because it will help everyone. If you benefit from the interaction (and likely you will), that's great, but that is not the point. The point is to help this world through all of your interactions. The best way to do that is to set aside your me-based thinking and look to benefit your organization as a whole.

Change your attitude, but remain natural.

Along those lines, you need to take a look at your attitude. This is not a "check yourself before you wreck yourself" approach where you no longer get to have any hard edges or character. It is a simple switch in view.

Often our view is that we want to look out for ourselves and only ourselves. Then, if we have any energy to consider others, we'll carve out a little time to do that. What that means is that we hoard all our kindness and compassion for ourselves, and we may occasionally smile at someone in the hallway to convince ourselves we are a good person.

If we want to experience the joy and lightness that comes from bodhicitta, we need to change our attitude. That means instead of hoarding our kindness and compassion, we must offer it at all times, to all beings. We are included in "all beings," so we don't need to stop being kind or compassionate to ourselves. The shift in view is from "I'm going to make samsara work for me" to "I'm going to work for all beings."

The second half of this slogan points out the way we should approach this transition in attitude—we should remain natural. There is a sense of relaxation in this statement. We should not get hyped up about trying to embrace all beings and kick ourselves when we shy away from absolute empathy. As we approach this switch in perspective, we should continue to offer ourselves the same wonderful qualities we are offering others.

Be grateful to everyone.

There are many reasons we should be grateful to everyone. The primary one is that everyone we encounter, hear about, or know of automatically signs up on the list of people we should try to benefit.

When you encounter someone competing with you for a job, that is a moment you can practice the Mahayana path. You can go in the door marked PASSION AGGRESSION IGNORANCE DANGER KEEP OUT and think up lots of ways to slander them when it is your time to apply for the position, or you can go in the MEDITATION AND VIRTUOUS ACTIVITY door and wish them well. In either case, you should be grateful to them, because they have given you the opportunity to practice breaking your habitual patterns and developing empathy.

Similarly, when you learn of someone who is doing things that you find atrocious, that is another time to practice compassion. Contemplate the idea that they are only trying to be happy, just like you. You can consider the six paramitas and determine which one you might be able to offer that person.

Along these lines, I would recommend taking on a new practice. It is very difficult, but it slices through habitual patterns like a sword through paper: stop complaining. In her book *Is Everyone Hanging Out Without Me? (And Other Concerns)*, my celebrity crush Mindy Kaling describes how Steve

Carell, her fellow actor on the TV show *The Office*, was notorious for not complaining. Despite Mindy's best efforts, Steve could never be enticed to complain about anything or anyone. And that quality inspired her to want to be the sort of person he admires. I love that story. Simply by not complaining, he brought out in others the desire to act in a virtuous way. Steve Carell's coworkers wanted to become better people simply because he would not complain.

I had never thought of this aspect of my speech until Sakyong Mipham Rinpoche gave a talk about it. I remember his advice clearly: complaining doesn't help anyone; it only furthers negativity. Instead of complaining, you should seek out solutions to whatever problems ail you. Plus, if all beings are actually practice opportunities, we shouldn't complain about them. We should be grateful for their existence!

Trungpa Rinpoche has said of this mind-training slogan, "If someone hurts you, you should be thankful to them for giving you the opportunity to practice."[2] I would add that you have the opportunity to practice even if someone doesn't hurt you. Everyone we encounter sparks the mentality of passion, aggression, or ignorance unless we can connect with a spacious mind and our bodhicitta. The choice of which route we take is up to us.

EMPTINESS + COMPASSION = POSITIVE CHANGE

In exploring the Mahayana principles of bodhicitta, virtue, karma, the six paramitas, and empathy, we can discover a life that is full of meaning. In order to infuse these principles with juice, we must realize on an experiential level a sense of emptiness.

Emptiness in the Buddhist context is not like a glass without water that we can point to and say, "It's empty." Emptiness is not based on the relative notion of fullness. It is a return to the teachings on prajna. The paramitas are so juicy because they are infused with that wisdom that knows the nature of reality, that has removed me-based thinking. When we step outside of our me-based reality, we enter one that is based in breaking down the dualistic barriers between ourselves and others. From that point of view, compassion can flow freely and we experience great joy.

You meditate to become truly familiar with yourself. As a result of that practice, you gradually step away from thinking only about yourself and then wake up to the fact that you do not exist in the way you think you do. An understanding of impermanence plays a part here. You can examine yourself and think about whether you are the exact same person you were ten years ago, a year ago, or even yesterday. Your experience, your body, and your knowledge are all changing moment by moment. You are not the stagnant, set human being you think you are.

By that same token, neither are our friends, coworkers, and family. Are they the same beings we always think them to be? They too are constantly changing, fluid beings. Emptiness, then, means that the world and all of us, its inhabitants, are not what we think they are. We are all actually ever-changing conglomerations of skin and bone and sweat and tears and thoughts and emotions. To take any of us seriously would be silly. With that in mind, emptiness can be viewed as an experience wherein we realize we can approach our life and world with an open heart and a sense of humor.

From this point of view, we can offer compassion and practice the Mahayana path without having to make a big deal out of it. We can relax and have a sense of lightness, as opposed to holding an uptight "OMG how am I going to save the world right now?" mentality. Combining our experience of emptiness with our experience of compassion allows us to fluidly engage with our environment and create positive change in the world around us.

In her book *The Top Five Regrets of the Dying,* Bronnie Ware describes the five biggest regrets of the patients she encountered during her years as a caregiver.[3] Surprisingly, the first one was "I wish I'd had the courage to live a life true to myself, not the life others expected of me."

When you practice the principles introduced thus far, you will live a life true to yourself. You can overcome other people's expectations and bravely engage in a lifetime journey of being aligned with your own moral compass, your awake heart. By living in accord with the practices of mindfulness and compassion, you have a much better shot at creating change that is meaningful, without forcing or changing major aspects of who you are. You don't have to work so hard at this idea; you can just let your bodhicitta naturally transform your environment. After all, the second biggest regret on that list was "I wish I hadn't worked so hard."

PART THREE

MAHAYANA

Six Tools for Compassionate Leadership

13 / BENEVOLENCE, OR BASHING AGGRESSION WITH THE VELVET HAMMER

The difference between a pebble and a mountain lies in whom you ask to move it.

—Marcus Buckingham

Growing up, I was always intrigued by the comic-book character Jamie Madrox, also known as the Multiple Man. When he was born, Jamie Madrox was slapped by the doctor and an instant duplicate of his body appeared. He was born with the superpower to create these duplicates at any time, and he shares both a telepathic and an empathetic connection with them. As a result, he can be in multiple places at any given time and can even lead multiple lives. At one point he sent a number of his duplicates out into the world to experience different lifestyles and then absorbed them back into his being, retaining their memories and experiences.

I think many of us would enjoy this ability. Imagine being able to live out multiple lives, never having to make a decisive choice about your career or in your personal life—you could do everything you wanted by sending out duplicate versions of yourself and then gaining their wisdom and memories. You could travel widely, run a farm, or pursue a dozen different careers, all by yourself.

The thing is, you and I don't have that superpower. At some point we have to acknowledge that we can't do everything we want to do or pursue every whim fully, because we can't be everywhere at once. We have to utilize our energy skillfully so that it feels like we are moving lots of pebbles instead of trying to move a mountain all at once. Furthermore, we need to realize that we can't do it all alone. If we want to do all the various things we aspire to do, we must play to our strengths while relying on others.

If you want to accomplish your various aspirations, there is no better way than to become a leader. Leaders serve in different ways in different contexts. There is the leader of a team, who takes on a project and makes sure others carry out the work needed to complete it. There are leaders of families, who bear the responsibility for making sure everyone is fed, clothed, and happy. There are leaders in the arts, the sciences, and every major industry—innovators who change the way that field looks forever.

A fundamental principle of leadership is that we need to engage others, work with their skill sets, and encourage the people with whom we collaborate. That involves leading others in a way that everyone feels good about. When you work with others in a supportive capacity, accomplishing goals you all believe in, you are leading in a mindful and compassionate manner. Even if you are not "the boss" in a given situation, you can act as a leader by manifesting the qualities of mindfulness and compassion and offering support to everyone you encounter.

There is a particular set of teachings in the Tibetan Buddhist canon that are geared toward leadership, known as the Six Ways of Ruling. Previously we talked about how to relate with a difficult boss. These teachings are about making sure you do not become that difficult boss. These six methods of leadership come under the Mahayana purview of working in a way that benefits everyone we meet. They show us how to bring our meditation practice off the cushion and lead others in a way that is in line with our own noble heart.

The earliest mention of these six principles of leadership is in a text by Jamgön Ju Mipham known as *The Way of the King*. Ju Mipham, also known as Mipham the Great, lived from 1846 to 1912 and was highly respected as someone who could take the esoteric teachings of Tibetan Buddhism and make them accessible to the world. The Six Ways of Ruling are based in the idea that we are all already the king.

For our purposes, we should not think of the term *king* as a male figure of royalty that lords over others based on what he thinks is best. Rather, the idea behind this term is that if you acknowledge your own basic goodness and worthiness, you are truly regal. You go through your day in a dignified and uplifted manner. You may not be in charge of a kingdom per se, but you can consider your home environment, your work environment, or your social environment in the same regal manner as a king would survey his land from his throne. There is a sense of taking ownership of your life. You can live in a way that has a profound effect on others, as your brilliance radiates out and is of benefit to the world as a whole.

Chögyam Trungpa Rinpoche, who brought the Shambhala teachings to the West, introduced the Six Ways of Ruling to his Western students, and his son and successor Sakyong Mipham Rinpoche has further explained them in his book *Ruling Your World*. These basic qualities, which anyone can practice and embody, are incredibly relevant to our modern-day workplace. The Six Ways of Ruling are about being benevolent, true, genuine, fearless, artful, and rejoicing.

They teach that each of us has the ability to lead others, once we develop a sense of confidence in our innate wisdom. That confidence is where the sense of regality comes from. Furthermore, the Six Ways of Ruling teach that you can be successful at leadership positions when you act primarily on behalf of others. Putting others' happiness before your own is a surefire way to earn the trust of your coworkers and creates fluid communication among everyone. This combination of conviction in your own goodness and empathy for your colleagues can manifest in a myriad of skillful ways that are worth celebrating.

From certainty in your own basic goodness, you can lead others in a manner that is just. A leader who is grounded in this form of confidence is often well regarded because people know them to be worthy of respect; they are looking out for others as much as they are looking out for themselves.

You may not necessarily desire a great leadership position, but when you engage your work with certainty in your own wisdom and a desire to be helpful, people are naturally drawn to you. They are magnetized to these qualities because these are the same qualities that they long for in their own lives. They want to work with you because they see that you are living a life that has purpose. When that occurs, leadership is a natural progression of your relationship.

A PATH OF SERVICE

Leadership in the Shambhala tradition is not an opportunity for personal gain. There is no room for selfishness in the Six Ways of Ruling. I recently met with a meditation student who expressed concern that she was being selfish in taking time away from her spouse to practice meditation in the morning. As we continued our discussion, it became clear that the term she was using wasn't the most accurate one. She wasn't being selfish; she was clearing out the time to take care of herself.

There is a fine line between being selfish—when your motivation is to do anything possible to make sure you come out on top—and taking care of yourself so you can be of assistance to others. You have to take care of yourself, or you can't continue to be helpful to others. No one is going to pat you on the back and say, "Good job; you really worked yourself to the bone there and are too exhausted to work tomorrow." While there is no room for selfishness in the Six Ways of Ruling, there is room for taking care of yourself.

You can spot good leaders because they are able to simultaneously take care of themselves while taking care of others. Good leaders are also humble. They long to be helpful to the people they work with, rather than assuming that those individuals will be subservient to them.

The view of leadership in Shambhala Buddhism is that it is a wonderful opportunity to serve others. It may not always feel wonderful; often it includes mind-numbing meetings and facing conflict a dozen times a day. Still, without these boring meetings and strong-minded colleagues, how could we develop all the great Buddhist qualities we want to cultivate?

JOINING HEAVEN AND EARTH

A leader in the Shambhala context knows that in order to be successful, you have to join the day-to-day details of earth with a larger vision for what could be, which is referred to as heaven. Earth is the knowledge that you have to meet the budgetary goals for the end of the month and diligently planning events every day to make sure that happens. Heaven is the knowledge that in ten years you'll see this particular month as just a stepping-stone toward doubling the size of your company or taking over a new field of industry. A strong leader can join these two, heaven and earth, and does not see them as conflicting. In other words, a leader can simultaneously hold a long-term vision and act in a way that accomplishes what needs to happen right now.

Not too long ago, I was surprised to encounter the best boss I ever had in the form of a twenty-five-year-old grad student named Liz McKenna. Even though she was younger than I was, she immediately commanded my respect because she proved she was able to simultaneously hold the large view of our community-organizing work while remaining sensitive to the details of my particular job. When her superiors dramatically shifted their expectations of us employees, she was able to articulate the logic of those changes while working with each of us on how we could alter the minutiae of our activity to skillfully reach our goals. She could represent the long-term vision we were trying to accomplish while respecting what it would take for each of us to realize that vision. Because she was able to join heaven and earth, she became known as a strong leader.

Marcus Buckingham, the best-selling author and founder of the leadership development platform Stand Out, once said, "If you want to understand leadership, you have to understand it through the impact a leader has on followers. The word *leadership* explodes into meaninglessness if you don't think about it from that perspective. What a leader does for followers is turn anxiety into confidence."[1]

A leader who cannot hold out a long-term vision and gets lost in the minutiae of a company is often lost in anxiety. This only inspires anxiety in the people they work with. A leader who only can hold a lofty ideal of what their workplace should look like comes off as unreliable and out of touch, which also inspires anxiety.

According to Marcus Buckingham and the Shambhala tradition, the best way to judge a leader is by analyzing the people whom he or she leads. If these individuals are mired in doubt, inefficient, and full of fear, then that is a rotten leader. However, if they have a connection to their own confidence, specifically confidence in their own wisdom and goodness, then that is a leader worth admiring, one who has inspired others to overcome their anxiety and be productive. That is a leader who can join heaven and earth. Their every task proceeds flawlessly like a pebble rolling down a slide.

The Six Ways of Ruling actually teach us how to undertake this joining of heaven and earth. The first of the six is known as benevolence.

THE BENEVOLENT LEADER

The Oxford English Dictionary defines *benevolent* as "well-meaning and kindly." In the context of the Six Ways of Ruling, however, benevolence means more than just meaning well; it is actively engaging kindness so that the lives of the people you are leading are changed for the better.

A leader who practices benevolence is naturally open and accommodating. They won't shoot down ideas that initially sound dumb; they are willing to hear others out and consider all options. This is because a benevolent leader is someone who has freed themselves from the bondage of caring only for their own welfare, and thus they have room in their heart for others. They are open to other people's perspectives and recognize other points of view.

One aspect of being accommodating is recognizing that people suffer. When you are leading a team, it is not enough to offer encouraging remarks and wish your colleagues well. You know very well how you suffer and thus can be very accommodating when you see others engaging in similar behavior patterns. You have to go beyond the dictionary meaning of *benevolent* and put yourself in other people's shoes by practicing empathy. For example, benevolence might mean that you are open enough to recognize that keeping employees late ruins last-minute dinner plans with their spouse or makes them less likely to get enough sleep to be competent the next day. Seeing their situation and feeling empathy will lead you to decide what is best for both the project at hand and the employees. You are taking a holistic look at your work situation rather than focusing on deadlines alone.

GENTLENESS AND HUMOR

When you are open to recognizing the suffering of others, you are more likely to embody other aspects of benevolence, such as gentleness and humor. You realize that you don't have to take your position and the pressures of serving in a leadership role so seriously. People's projections about what ought to happen will come up, and gentleness and humor will end up being your best tools for combating everyday confusion and aggression in the workplace.

My friend Liza runs a company that consults, tracks, and mentors fashion tech start-ups. When I first got to know her, I asked about the difficulty of working with so many start-ups; surely she must encounter aggression and disappointment in her line of work. She revealed to me that she had actually earned a somewhat humorous nickname: The Velvet Hammer. Apparently Liza is often in the position of telling clients that they will not get what they want, but because she is benevolent—because she is gentle yet firm and offers her sense of humor—people always seem to respect and like her.

When you have to face a confrontation in the office, keep the image of a velvet hammer in mind. The hammer is a tool that accomplishes what needs to get done. Yet the velvet makes it soft, gentle, and thus people are more likely to respect it. As a velvet hammer, you don't have to back down from the aggression you face, but you don't have to buy into whatever story line someone tries to sell you either. You can overcome aggression with this perfect blend of gentle conviction and the soft touch of humor.

When you feel you want to lean into aggression, I recommend you practice benevolence through being just as kind as you would want to be irate. When you feel like lashing out at someone, consider just how angry you are feeling on a scale of one to ten. Then consider what your reaction would be if you were that same number on a scale of gentleness.

For example, if you are presenting a plan you think is brilliant and a naysayer interrupts with an objection, you might want to shut them up with a snide retort. Maybe that's a three on the aggression scale. If you were to transmute that aggressive three into a gentleness three, instead you might ask that person a few questions, allowing them to express their concerns before moving on.

A leader who is benevolent knows that aggression helps no one. Aggression is a shovel with which you dig your own grave. Give it up and instead try gentleness and humor.

Once in a while I receive an e-mail from someone who is vehemently against whatever I am working on. It could be a project for a nonprofit or something I have written. In general, my practice is to offer gentleness and humor to those individuals as I open up the lines of communication with them.

However, there is one fellow who, before my first book even came out, was convinced that it was misguided and an insult to our shared Buddhist lineage. At first, I practiced gentleness and humor with this person, openly acknowledging that I am just as prone to mistakes as anyone, if not more so. In fact, I am always open to the fact that my mistakes are my greatest teachers. If the book turned out to be a mistake, I was sure I would know it pretty quickly, so I suggested that we should be patient and see what happens.

Thankfully, the book was well received, and shortly after it came out, I began to receive letters regularly from people claiming that it was helpful to their life and to their meditation practice. Still, this one individual (who I am guessing has still not read the book) continued to write me every few weeks to say that what I am doing is pretty awful.

After the first few months of this, I decided that one way to practice gentleness to myself and to him was to give him a lot of space. Often when you offer space to someone, their aggression naturally fizzles. You are not pouring fuel on the fire of their anger, and without it, the heat of aggression gradually fades out.

After nine months of giving him space, though, I had to realize that this guy was going to keep being verbally abusive. I began to plan all sorts of snappy responses to him. I composed a dozen e-mails to him in my head, all of which I thought might finally shut him up.

Then I remembered a tale of two monks who were walking together. As they approached a river, they saw a woman who was struggling to cross it. The elder monk said to her, "Here, jump on my back, and I will carry you across." The woman was grateful and the two monks waded into the water. At the other shore, the woman jumped off the elder monk and the two men walked on in silence.

The younger monk was furious. He felt that the elder monk had broken his monastic vows by acting so carelessly with a woman. He steamed and steamed over this for hours until finally he exploded: "How could you violate our precepts like that?"

The older monk took a moment to figure out what he was referring to, and then understood. "Are you still angry about me carrying that woman?" he asked. "I left her on the shore hours ago, but because of your anger, you have been carrying her this entire time."

After I recalled this story, I realized how silly it was for me to be angry at this abusive person. His words only carried the weight I allow them to carry. Once I was able to drop the story lines around him and our dynamic, genuine compassion welled up in me. I was able to see how he was suffering, and my heart genuinely went out to him. Then I was able once again to practice gentleness with him and have a sense of humor about the situation. He may continue to be angry, but I remembered that I do not have to continue to be affected by that aggression. I did not need to carry him around with me like the young monk and his anger.

One way to practice benevolence in a case like this is to take a moment to recognize that all parties concerned have at least one thing in common: basic goodness. The Sakyong has said, "When you connect with someone on the basis of both of your inherent worthiness there is a different dynamic that is taking place."[2] Instead of meeting someone on the battlefield of aggression, you can meet them in the spacious playground of shared innate wisdom.

You may not be able to be everywhere at once, but you can work with others to make a significant change in your world, or at least your organization. Being open, accommodating, and gentle and offering your sense of humor are all ways you can join the details of your daily routine with the long-term vision for what you hope to accomplish. You may not be the Multiple Man, but you can work with multitudes of men and women in a benevolent manner. You can be a benevolent leader and, when faced with aggression, bash through it with the gentleness of a velvet hammer.

14 / TRUE, OR HOW TO BE STEADY AS A MOUNTAIN

In matters of style, swim with the current; in matters of principle, stand like a rock.

— *Thomas Jefferson*

It's a familiar scene in old Western movies: a sheriff stands in the middle of the street, staring down the bandit who is looking to take over his town. They are but paces apart, each about to reach for their gun, and the only detectable difference is that the bandit's eyes seem to flicker back and forth from his gun to the sheriff to the crowd, while the sheriff remains unmoving. In these scenes, the sheriff always wins.

The second of the Six Ways of Ruling is known as true. True, in the Shambhala Buddhist tradition, is not about always telling the truth. That is a good start to living a life that is true, sure, but it is not the whole story. Chögyam Trungpa Rinpoche did say, at one point, "If you are telling the truth, then you can speak gently, and your words will have power."[1]

Breaking down that simple statement reveals a few things. The first is that when you speak the truth, you can aim to practice gentleness, an aspect of benevolence. Benevolence is the foundation of the qualities of true. Through gentleness and the directness of speaking a true statement, you are giving weight to your words. You are giving them power by allowing the qualities of true to shine forth.

Truth can be subjective, though, right? One man's truth may lead him to believe that he is fighting for the freedom of his country. Another man may perceive that individual as a terrorist. That is his truth. When we talk about being true in the Shambhala context, we should be clear that the term does not refer to insisting on the truth of a particular opinion or idea. True, in this context, means being true to the view of basic goodness. That is something that we can all experience; it is a unifying quality we can all touch and get to know. Really being true, then, simply means being in tune with your core wisdom. It is a sense of conviction that you are basically good, and others are basically good, and you can move forward from that understanding.

When you have conviction in basic goodness, you develop a sense of weightiness, like the sheriff. He knows that he is doing what is right, what needs to be done, so he is stable and solid, like a mountain. Being true to your own goodness has that kind of power. You can be as steadfast as a mountain when you experience the strength of your basic goodness.

I recently read a study that reported that the millennial generation switches between various devices and forms of media (laptops, smart phones, television, and so on) an average of twenty-seven times per hour. That means that their attention span cannot be more than a few minutes. They have habituated themselves to multitasking, thinking that is a smart way to be in the world and accomplish a number of things.

It's widely believed today that you should multitask in order to be efficient. People pride themselves on their ability to answer text messages while churning out reports while on the phone with a client, as if doing all these things in a half-present manner were praiseworthy. A Buddhist friend once asked me if I ever had my computer out while the television was on.

Guiltily, I admitted I did sometimes split my attention between the two. "That's great! Two-screen entertainment!" he happily exclaimed, as if this were the wave of the future.

I hate to disagree with my friend, but I think if you want to lead others, you need to let go of the notion that you can do everything at once. You need to focus, bringing yourself fully to whatever task is at hand or meeting is taking place, rather than strategizing about all the other things you could be doing.

An Unwavering Presence

Olympic athletes provide a good example of this kind of focus. When I watch an Olympic swimmer or gymnast, I can't help marveling at their incredible presence and power. They are not trained in splitting their attention between multiple electronic devices and media twenty-seven times an hour. They have devoted years to becoming one-pointed at very specific tasks. I don't think we appreciate Olympians because they are the best at doing multiple things in a short period; their power rests in their unwavering presence.

My friend Ericka runs the Shambhala Center in New York City. I first met her when she was in event planning, then later I worked with her more closely when I served as the center's interim director and she served as my number two. During that time I was impressed by her steadiness. We sat across from each other for months and would jokingly keep track of who would handle which difficult conversations that came our way.

The receptionist would buzz our shared office and say, "Oliver is on the line and has some questions." We would shoot each other a knowing look, acknowledging that Oliver would likely monopolize the better part of an hour if given the chance. Ericka would often very kindly take the bullet and speak with difficult individuals like him.

I never worried about letting Ericka take these calls because she really understands the nature of being true to your own goodness. She would be completely charming and nice to

Oliver, exhibiting the second of the Six Ways of Ruling. No matter what he would say to try to unhinge Ericka, she always held her seat. She was constantly true to her conviction in her goodness, as well as the goodness of the demanding person she was encountering.

When it came time to hire the next executive director of the Shambhala Center, she was an obvious choice. Even in her interviews for the position she was able to bring a sense of weightiness to the conversation. There was tremendous power in her being, because she was so in tune with her experience of basic goodness. People would pose very hard questions to her, and she would remain as steady as a mountain as she delivered her answers. She was unshakable.

Having watched Ericka in her executive position over the last few years, I have realized that one element of being true is always acting from that sense of confidence. True is not puffing up your ego to think you're the best or better than anyone. It is confidence that everyone possesses basic goodness and that therefore you will be able to resolve whatever issue arises.

When you are true to yourself in this way, you spontaneously act with integrity. There is something about you that comes across as completely sane. That mountain-like steadiness is apparent to everyone, and they see that you will not flinch at the light breeze of other people's neuroses. There is something so reliable about that; people grow to trust you as a result.

Think about the company you keep in your social life. Are you attracted to people who are unreliable? When you sit down with someone to catch up about your love lives or mutual friends, do you secretly wish that they would keep checking their phone for text messages? Or do you find yourself more attracted to friends who are steady as a mountain?

Often our best friends are the ones who are unconditionally there for us. When we sit down with them, they are genuinely present, inquisitive and responsive to what is going on. They are the people we can lean on in times of need because their support is unwavering. That is a true friend.

NATURAL DIPLOMACY

In both friendship and in leadership, being true is related to diplomacy. This is not the diplomacy of brokering peace negotiations or playing secretary of state. Diplomacy here means that we are true to our inherent power, that steadiness of the sheriff or the mountain, and this leads to natural tact and skill. There is a sense of ease in working with people when we are true.

We have natural diplomacy because we understand how power works. We are not looking to wield it in order to get ahead of everyone and be the best at everything. Instead, we know that power is best used when everyone profits from it—when we share it and empower others. True power, in this sense, is that you can see what people need in any given moment, and because you are true they trust you are acting on their behalf. That is integrity. That is leadership you can feel good about.

There is a form of charisma that occurs naturally when you give rise to the quality of true. In *The Charisma Myth,* Olivia Fox Cabane argues that charismatic behavior can be broken down into three basic elements: presence, power, and warmth.

You can be charismatic if you master these three elements, each of which is related to the second of the Six Ways of Ruling. The first aspect of being true is unwavering presence, that mountain-like steadiness. Then there is the second aspect: power. There is tremendous power within that steadiness, that Olympian ability to truly be there for a task or for others. The last element Fox Cabane mentions is warmth.

When we consider the image of a mountain in relation to the quality of true, we are not thinking of a barren wasteland. It is not a cold, snow-covered mountain that no one would ever want to visit. It is a lush landscape, full of trees, wildflowers, and beautiful rocks and boulders. The mountain is warm and inviting. People want to visit this mountain because it is a pleasant place to be.

When we watch an Olympic athlete perform, we yearn for them to do their best. This is an interesting phenomenon at sporting events. Normally, there is an athlete or a team whom we want to succeed. That team becomes "us." Because we want *us* to win, their competition, some other team, transforms into the *them* we want to see defeated. More often than not, sporting events embody this us-versus-them dynamic. In other words, they perpetuate aggression.

After watching the Olympics, I have come to believe that the athletes all share these three elements of presence, power, and warmth. I mention that because, regardless of their country of origin, many people find themselves rooting for these athletes simply because of their incredible charisma. We want them to succeed because they are exhibiting this quality of being true, which eliminates the dualistic element often seen in sports.

In the same regard, when you think of being true, you should not consider yourself as standoffish or apart from others. When you are true, there is no *them* that we need to conquer or subjugate; there is only us. Perhaps the most important aspect of being true to your own goodness is that you exhibit to others that confidence in your core being. You share yourself freely, so others feel invited to work with you in an authentic manner. That is true warmth.

Olivia Fox Cabane observes that we may think we can fake these qualities. "We may think that we can fake listening. But we're wrong. When we're not fully present in an interaction, people will see it. Our body language sends a clear message that other people read and react to, at least on a subconscious level."[2] People do not want to be around someone who is false or does not truly care about being with them. Part of cultivating the quality of true is being true to others and being fully there with them.

When you devote yourself to being true, you are connecting with the most intimate part of who you are and putting it on display. You are making your basic goodness available to those you work with, and they will likely be inspired to see that. As you exhibit the steadfast presence, the stable power, and the genuine warmth of being true, people will grow to trust and respect you. You will be able to lead with skill, supported by your coworkers and colleagues.

15 / GENUINE, OR POINTING TO THE STARS

Imagine taking your entire company out into a wide-open field just after twilight. You all lie down on your backs, and, as the first stars appear, you point to one and say "There. That's a star." Likely no one would interject and say, "No! That's an air conditioner." Because it is obvious you are all seeing the same thing, a star, you all can appreciate it without contention.

The image of pointing to a star illustrates the third of the Six Ways of Ruling: genuine. Having developed the qualities of benevolence, such as patience, gentleness, and humor, and the various aspects of being true, including power, presence, and warmth, you are naturally prepared to be genuine. Genuine in this sense is not just being clear and direct. It involves pointing out the exact nature of things. You are pointing to reality in an indisputable manner. When you do this correctly, you may as well be pointing to a star in the sky—it is that clear. You are not representing your own personal state of being genuine but instead the way things genuinely are or could be.

Genuine is based in knowing what is in your mind and heart, which is true, and not being afraid of it. We can genuinely be who we are. We can genuinely lead others in a way that everyone appreciates. We can even genuinely make mistakes. All of this is okay when it is rooted in our innate goodness.

The analogy of pointing at a star in the sky illustrates that there is something very logical about being genuine. Genuine is pointing out whatever truth exists behind mixed expectations or set opinions. A star is a star. It is hard to argue otherwise. When you are genuine, you are able to discern what needs to happen in any given moment, based on the wisdom of your own understanding. That truth is the truth, and if it's presented in the right way, it also is hard to argue with.

Thus, one aspect of being genuine in the context of the Six Ways of Ruling is pointing out the irrefutable logic behind a situation. If you are in a meeting and are in touch with your own basic goodness, it becomes easier to discern what needs to happen. You can speak up and point to that simple truth just like you might point at a star. If you are being genuine, people will likely not jump down your throat; they will look at your proposal just as they would a star and say, "Ah. I see that. I have a hard time finding fault with that."

In some sense, genuine is merely pointing out the reality of any given moment. It is highlighting your own wisdom and creating a map for others to discover their own.

When I took my first position out of college, I was twenty-two years old and, as I've noted, from a conventional point of view I was unqualified to run the nonprofit organization I was in charge of. It was no surprise that its senior members took it upon themselves to question my logic at every turn.

If I made a minor decision like deciding to offer a certain type of class more frequently than in the past, I immediately got feedback. After announcing our program schedule by e-mail, I would receive a reply within minutes from a gentleman who sounded slightly cantankerous: "We need to meet about this."

In the spirit of benevolence, I always agreed to meet with him. Walking into the meeting, I would try to embody the quality of true, taking my seat in a mountain-like manner, rooted in conviction in our shared basic goodness. Then this gentleman would go on at length about why we had always offered the previous number of classes and not this new number, and how we would never find people to staff those classes, and how we would never get enough people to take these classes, and on and on.

I would listen patiently, and when it was my turn to speak, I would address each of his objections succinctly, holding in my mind the image of pointing to a star I would point out the logic behind the increased number of classes, roping in figures from recent events that showed that we could support them, in terms of both participants and staff, and highlighting our new marketing efforts. Slowly, meticulously, point by point, I mapped out the logic behind why I was doing what I was doing. Once that was apparent, this gentleman always relented and came to understand and support my efforts.

To me, that was the most amazing part of our meetings. He would come in very grumpy, but because I applied the first three ways of ruling, he left feeling very good about our situation. Once the logic was shown in detail, he could see that there was nothing to be grumpy about, and those feelings would dissipate. That is the power of being genuine.

It was, in some sense, a great test of my work. When founding the Institute for Compassionate Leadership, I went through many rounds with focus groups, detailing the entirety of my business plan. I always picked the sharpest minds I could find in my Rolodex. If my logic could not hold up under someone else's scrutiny, then I wasn't pointing to the reality of the situation. I might have thought I was being genuine, but perhaps I was being genuine to my personal interpretation and not to the situation as a whole. I might as well have been pointing to a star and saying it was a cloud or a rainbow.

Having to consider the logic behind the work I did was very helpful in this way. It allowed me to discern whether the actions I was taking to found the organization were in line with the Six Ways of Ruling as well as reality overall. If not, then I needed to try something else. If so, my staff and active volunteers would come away satisfied, knowing I was working in everyone's best interests.

Working with Intimidation

There are times, however, when your being genuine can actually intimidate others. When you are genuine, you are offering other people the opportunity to meet you in that state of mind. You are opening the door to the reality of what is going on, which is not always pretty. You are highlighting the fact that other people may not be considering the big picture or being genuine in relating to the project overall. If they are bullshitting their way through work, your genuine presence only illuminates that fact. As such, they may not always appreciate having their bullshit put on display.

Similarly, if you are lost in your own sense of the way things should be, and not realizing the way they are, then you are merely displaying your ideas and opinions, which is not necessarily genuine either. In this case, you may mean well, but you yourself are engaging in bullshit. Someone may come along and, because they embody this third aspect of the Six Ways of Ruling, highlight your own inability to see the big picture genuinely.

Chögyam Trungpa Rinpoche pointed out that we should not be deterred in our genuineness, even if it does make other people uncomfortable. In his commentary on the lojong slogans, he said, "Our genuineness has to be shared with someone. It has to be given up. . . . We have to give our genuineness away to someone."[1] If you do not offer your genuine presence, your impact as a leader is not as powerful as it potentially could be. By offering your genuineness, even in uncomfortable positions or when you are calling people out, you are offering them the chance to follow your lead and act in the same manner. That is an offering that we all can enjoy.

You know how it feels when you are not genuine. Often, it feels like you are living half a life. You are more prone to distraction, and you aren't truly happy. I believe that no one wants to live like this. We long to be genuine but have not habituated ourselves to it. Will Durant, summarizing Aristotle, said, "We are what we repeatedly do."[2] If you continue to repeat days when you are not your most authentic you, when you do not practice the Six Ways of Ruling, then that is who you end up becoming.

Durant, summarizing Aristotle again, said, "Excellence then, is not an act, but a habit." Excellence in the workplace is not a onetime thing. Neither is being genuine. In both cases, you have to repeatedly come back to the idea that you want to be genuine with others. If you can hold that as a mantra worth repeating, then you can spend your day coming back to this simple principle over and over again, gradually undoing negative habitual patterns and replacing them with the Six Ways of Ruling.

GIVING UP GENUINENESS

Chögyam Trungpa Rinpoche has also encouraged us to give up our genuineness. One aspect of this teaching points to the idea that being genuine actually has nothing to do with us. Being genuine is not about being smarter than others or having the best plan or the most important insights. It is that we are able to see a clear course of action and point to it. Pointing out the logic behind a situation is always about benefiting others.

When you are genuine, you make things easier for others. This is actually very simple. You are in tune with who you are, and thus are not lost in your own neurotic garbage. Your mind is clear. It is not lost in the haze of "I need to get something out of this situation" or "I need to prove myself."

Because your mind is clear, it can clearly perceive the situation at hand. You can then genuinely offer what you see. Because others are often lost in their own hang-ups and fantasies, they may be slow to figure out the obvious logic for a task or project and will probably be grateful to you for pointing it out. That is what is meant by giving up genuineness: since it does not belong to us, we are readily available to offer it to the world at large.

MANTRA EXERCISE FOR AUTHENTICITY

For some of my meditation practices I use a *mala*, a string of beads for counting repetitions of a phrase or action. Often malas are used to count mantras.

In Tibetan Buddhist practice, mantras are Sanskrit phrases, sounds or words that can be recited to provoke inner change. *Mantra* is a Sanskrit word that can be translated as "to protect the mind." When someone recites a mantra, they are engaging in a meditation practice that cuts through harmful habitual patterns and focuses their attention on a more noble aspiration, thus protecting their mind from negativity and fortifying it with virtue.

One such mantra practice in Tibetan Buddhism is reciting OM MANI PADME HUM. This six-syllable mantra is associated with Avalokiteshvara, the bodhisattva of compassion. Each syllable carries a great deal of meaning. Generally, I recommend that people interested in actual mantra practice make a formal commitment to the Buddhist path and work closely with a qualified teacher who can explain the meanings of various mantras.

The idea of protecting our mind in this way is a good one, and we can use it as the basis for an informal recitation exercise. We should all aspire to protect our mind, fortifying it with virtue. Part of practicing the Six Ways of Ruling involves slicing off the me-based thinking that we often carry around and instead working for the benefit of others. One way to do that is to engage in a more personal, informal type of practice that feels true to ourselves. We can look to actual mantra practice as the basis of this particular exercise.

Malas come in many different forms. The traditional mala used in formal practice has 108 beads, but there are also wrist malas that have only 21. Sometimes when I am traveling, or even for my morning commute, I grab one of these malas and bring it with me.

I leave my formal mantra recitation practice for my time on the meditation cushion, but as I go through my travels and find myself lost in me-based thinking, I find it helpful to take out my mala discreetly and count out a few cycles of a reminder that strikes me as needed at that time. This is not a formal Buddhist practice but a more personal way to remind myself to move away from being lost in my own head.

For example, if you are at work and someone is giving you a hard time, it might be helpful to take out a mala and silently recite and contemplate the word *patience* 108 times. With each recitation, you can reflect on what the word means to you and what it means in this context. In taking the time to do that, you are slicing through the story line that surrounds your frustration and instead turning your attention to a quality you want to cultivate.

You don't have to make a big deal out of this informal exercise. In fact, the more discreet it is, the better. You shouldn't feel the need to show off how spiritual you are by waving your mala in people's faces; just practice for your own good, and thus for the good of others. This is an exercise that is best done in private, or at least not done in a flashy way. If you want to walk around your neighborhood and practice it, that is okay too. More often than not, people will be too lost in their own drama of the moment to even notice.

Before you begin, choose the phrase that makes the most sense to you as an antidote to whatever emotional disturbance you're currently experiencing. If you notice that you are lost in your own melodrama, you could recite the phrase *Come back to the present,* or if you are on your way to meet someone you have a hard time with, you could recite *kindness* as a reminder to treat them gently and with consideration. As you count your repetitions, reflect on the meaning of the word or phrase, coming back to that just as you come back to the breath during shamatha practice.

Whenever you engage in this practice, take a moment at the end of your recitation to raise your gaze and rest with whatever feeling has arisen.

The Six Ways of Ruling are based in preserving our connection to our innate wisdom, and that is hard to do when you find yourself bombarded by negativity or obstacles. As we continue to explore these tools for leadership, you may find it helpful to have a recitation counter of this sort with you. To take the time to count recitations of *benevolence, gentleness, presence,* or *warmth* may bring you back to the present moment and your connection with your basic goodness. From that point, you are returning to your most authentic you, and you can continue to practice being genuine.

16 / FEARLESSNESS, OR BEING DECISIVE IN AN INDECISIVE WORLD

Believe, don't fear, believe.

—*Olympic gold medal–winning gymnast Gabby Douglas*

The Six Ways of Ruling are divided into two broad categories: just and powerful. The first three principles—benevolent, true, and genuine—are about manifesting in a way that feels just when working with others. The next three qualities fall under the heading of powerful. All six embody the Mahayana aspiration of helping all beings we encounter.

In the Shambhala tradition, it is said that the way to wield power well is to wield it for the good of all. That is what it means to be powerful. It does not matter how much wealth you accumulate or how many titles you hold; true power comes from working for the welfare of others. That is the type of power we all can respect.

Some people who have power have poor judgment when it comes to knowing what to do with it. They make selfish decisions, or promote people for the wrong reasons, or create an environment where there is little room for praise or celebration. These sorts of leaders are the antithesis of what we should aspire to. Having seen these sorts of leaders, we can determine that we want to pursue leadership in a different way and practice the discipline to follow through on that belief.

According to the Six Ways of Ruling, power is not about waiting for someone to tap us on the shoulder and say, "It's your turn. Go be a powerful leader." We can express our power at any time. It comes from rooting ourselves in mindfulness and empathy, developing certainty in our basic nature, and acting from that conviction to help the world. When we combine all those things, we are naturally powerful.

One aspect of working from a position of power is learning when you need to be fearless. Fearlessness is the fourth of the Six Ways of Ruling, and the first of the three under the heading of powerful. That is because incredible energy and strength can come from approaching life in a fearless manner.

Fearlessness is not about ignoring fear or running away from it—quite the opposite. Fearlessness is about looking at our fear, learning it well, and seeing our way through it. We must become familiar with our fear if we want to experience fearlessness.

A few years ago, I was out on the town with a couple of people, happily chatting during a cab ride on our way to a party. Our taxi driver was distracted. He kept poking his head out the window as he drove. Perhaps the driver in the oncoming lane was distracted as well. As our driver sped up to rush through a yellow light, the car coming toward us tried to take a quick left turn. We crashed dramatically. Thankfully, we all walked away alive; the worst of it was that one friend had to endure a bit of surgery.

For all the following year, I was terrified to get into a taxi. If you have ever been in a New York City cab, you may understand why. Even without the trauma of surviving an accident, many people are nervous riding around in the constantly swerving, lane-switching traffic of the city. If you have never been to New York but you have played an obnoxious round of the video game Super Mario Kart, you can picture the scene pretty well.

However, I was not prepared to give up riding in cabs just

because I'd experienced fear. Saying, "Okay, I'm done with cabs" would not have been the best thing to do. Instead, I turned to the traditional Shambhala Buddhist teachings on fearlessness.

Fearlessness is based in the idea that in order to truly deal with your phobias, you need to confront them with an open heart and mind. Eventually, through repetition, meditation, and possibly even therapy, you can work through them. In my case, that meant getting back on the proverbial horse and continuing to navigate New York in cabs, breathing through my nervousness over and over again until my fear gradually faded.

FEAR ON THE MEDITATION CUSHION

Fear is powered by story lines, and fearlessness is powered by innate goodness. The former comes and goes; the other is a part of us. Meditation is a particularly useful tool for working with fear, because as we sit down to practice it, the same story lines and rough emotions come up constantly.

Every moment you sit on the meditation cushion is an opportunity to work with fear. It could be the fear of job insecurity, or the fear that you are not doing what you want to be doing with your life, or the fear that you are not good enough at any given thing. When those fears come up, the instruction is to label them *thinking* and return our attention to our breathing.

Often fear is not beaten back that easily. Sometimes you may find that within seconds of labeling a fear-based thought and coming back to your breath, the emotion arises again in the form of a different story line. The instruction is to continue to label these emotional story lines as *thinking* and come back to the breath.

If that does not work, another method is to drop the story line and just feel the emotion in your body. This may mean taking a two- or three-minute break from formal shamatha practice. Drop the various "Well, this could happen" or "They are definitely going to do this to me" dialogues playing out in your head, and just try to locate the fear within your body. Is your fear manifesting as tightness in your chest? Is it a rumbling in your head? Is it held within your arms? Your legs? Try to identify where the emotion resides.

Next, take a moment to contemplate the nature of the fear itself. Is your fear hot or cold? What color is your fear? Does it have a shape? A texture? As you ask yourself these questions, taking thirty seconds to a minute for each one, just let whatever answers arise come up and roll across your mind. Don't fixate on them or try to come up with an answer that seems right. Let them arise and pass like leaves floating in the wind.

At the end of the few minutes you have allotted for this contemplation, return to the formal shamatha meditation practice you normally do. At the end of your entire meditation session, notice if your fear feels as real as it did when you first sat down. More often than not, contemplations like this point out how ephemeral these emotional states actually are. We end up feeling more liberated, knowing that our fear is not as solid and real as it initially appeared.

If you encounter fear off the meditation cushion (and I am guessing you do), you can still engage in that simple contemplation practice. When I was working with the fear of riding in New York taxi cabs, this process was extremely helpful. If you are a nervous traveler or have an important meeting coming up, taking a few minutes to work through a contemplation like this may prove invaluable to your well-being.

Overcoming Hesitancy

As you become familiar with fear, you discover that you hold the ability to let it wash over you and walk through its fog into the brilliant and clear space of fearlessness. The story lines that are associated with fear will continue to come up in your life, but you always have the choice not to get hooked by them and instead reside in your fearless state, your own basic goodness.

Fearlessness, in this sense, is a condition in which you no

longer have any doubt about your innate wisdom. You can be fearless about jumping into that wisdom and swimming in its refreshing waters. As the Sakyong wrote in *Ruling Your World,* "Fear is a state of mind. Fearlessness is our nature." It is much better to rest in our nature than to engage a state of mind that only causes us suffering.

One way fear manifests at work is through extreme hesitancy. When you are disconnected from your own basic goodness, you have cut yourself off from your inner voice. You cannot make decisions based on the principle of being true to your wisdom, because you are too fearful to trust that it even exists.

One way fearlessness manifests at work is through freedom from hesitancy. If you can move beyond uncertainty in your basic goodness, then you can move beyond hesitation in making whatever decisions need to be made. When you face tough decisions, there will only be yes and no. There are not a lot of maybes when you are fearless, because you are genuine and thus you see the logic behind why things need to happen. Having determined the logical way forward, you know you ought to act decisively, and you feel the impetus to follow through on that logic. That is fearlessness at work.

Furthermore, if you act indecisively, you are only inspiring others to question your decision-making ability. This is not to say that you should lead from a sense of false confidence and just proclaim decisions for the sake of getting things done. That would only delay the questioning of your decision-making ability.

Instead, if you are connected to the first three of the Six Ways of Ruling, you can lead from a place of confidence in your goodness, in what is good for others, and in the logical path forward. You will inspire confidence in others through this form of leadership, as opposed to waffling on whether your decisions are the right ones and inspiring doubt. This is the methodical aspect of fearlessness: you are efficient in your work and others appreciate your bold decisions.

NOT KNOWING WHAT WILL HAPPEN NEXT

Still, even if we act in a fearless, decisive manner, there will be times when things do not go our way. You may lead a team to pitch a partnership to one company with their CEO in mind, but at the last minute that individual is called away and you're left pitching to her CFO, a very different person with very different expectations. I believe you can still ride the waves of uncertainty in a case like this through working with the Six Ways of Ruling, and fearlessness is especially important here.

Pema Chödrön once said, "A warrior accepts that we can never know what will happen to us next." She is referring to the bodhisattva, that openhearted warrior who lives life in a way that is full of compassion. If you aim to be a compassionate leader, the best thing to do is acknowledge that you will never know how things will work out. Fearlessness in the face of uncertainty is a powerful weapon for good.

As I mentioned earlier, I volunteer at a homeless aid organization called the Reciprocity Foundation. What sets Reciprocity apart from similar organizations in New York is that they try to meet each young student who comes through their doors in a way that caters to who they are and who they want to become. The students range from teenagers to young adults in their twenties. The methods employed vary from counseling to meditation instruction to massage to mentorship and job placement.

The students at Reciprocity are the sweetest, kindest human beings in New York City. Yet they have had incredibly hard lives. Many have felt unsafe or unwanted growing up or were abandoned at some point. They continue to face fear on the streets of New York every day, at constant risk of violence and rape. Yet they have learned that they cannot run from these experiences; they need to face them with bravery and, as much as possible, an open heart. One student recently said, "I've been abused so much on the streets. I could have easily been killed. I'm grateful for being alive." Many of us do not address fear in this straightforward manner, finding appreciation in our very being. Their example is inspiring.

Any time I consider working with fear, I reflect on the example of the students at Reciprocity Foundation. I imagine some of them may find it ironic that I look up to them, since supposedly I am a mentor there. Still, the fact that they can exhibit their basic goodness and innate wisdom, despite the fear they face on a regular basis, continues to amaze me.

They are warriors who have accepted that they cannot know what will happen next in their lives. Yet they strive to make the best of their situation. More than any role model or superhero, these youths are consistently fearless. We could all learn a lot by following their lead.

Each of us has our own set of fears. To believe that we can retreat up into an ivory tower and hide from them for the rest of our lives is foolish and only fans the fires that fear depends on. In order to overcome the hold that fear has on us, we need to confront it fully. Doing so, we end up kinder, more compassionate, and more open to helping others through their fear. This is our path.

Fear will always arise in new forms as we go about our lives. To embrace it when it arises not as obstacle but as journey is a brilliant learning experience. From this, we can help others do the same. Once we recognize that our natural state is basically fearless, we can inspire confidence in others.

17 / ARTFULNESS, OR ARRANGING YOUR KINGDOM

I'm not the smartest fellow in the world, but I can sure pick smart colleagues.

—*Franklin D. Roosevelt*

Ruling our work situation is an art, not a science. When I was preparing for my first major work position after college, a friend told me a story about Henry Ford, the man who founded the Ford Motor Company. Apparently, despite all of his engineering smarts, Henry Ford was not a brilliant businessman when he was young.

The story goes that at his first major press conference for Ford Motors, he invited reporters into his office to ask him about any aspect of his business. One by one the reporters would step up and pose very specific questions about the company. "Can you explain how your third-quarter sales compare to your first two quarters?" someone would ask, and Henry would nod, then push a button on his desk. In would walk a man who handled his finances, and he would explain their sales reports. When another reporter asked about how his employees were treated, Henry would nod and push another button, and in would walk someone who would talk about the company from a human resources point of view. The entire press conference proceeded in that manner, with various trusted officials coming in to explain the company on behalf of Henry Ford.

I am not entirely sure if that story is actually true (and, after all, Henry himself famously said, "History is more or less bunk"), but the principle behind it seems to be. Henry Ford knew his strengths and weaknesses, and he worked skillfully with others based on that knowledge. Franklin Roosevelt, according to the epigraph of this chapter, also had this ability to pick colleagues whose strengths would balance out his own weak points. As a result, these leaders are examples of people who were known for being artful.

Artfulness is the fifth of the Six Ways of Ruling. It is the ability to flow with your life, as opposed to measuring it out in exact terms. It is seeing what needs to happen and making it happen, utilizing the skill sets at your disposal. When you are successful at being artful, everything looks effortless.

In order to truly be artful, you have to manifest a genuine presence. If you practice the first three ways of ruling discussed thus far, then you are already in touch with and acting from your own goodness. You are already presenting your most authentic self. As a result, people will be drawn to you. We all want to work with someone who is being authentic, who perceives situations clearly, and who we trust will put us to work in the manner most befitting our skills. That is when artfulness matters the most.

THE RIGHT PEOPLE FOR THE RIGHT POSITIONS

My friend Arshad has served as the CEO of a number of small businesses over the last decade. It seems like every time I see him, he is working away on another start-up or helping someone else with their business. As a result, he is constantly hiring people. He has been able to identify his own strengths and the strengths of the people he works closely with, and then discern how to bring in other people with skills that would balance theirs. Based on the number of projects I have seen him pull off, he is quite good at this aspect of being artful.

The other day I caught up with him and asked about his approach to selecting people to work with. Like other human resource pros, Arshad looks for the qualities in a potential hire. He asks himself, "Is this person reliable? Are they communicative? Can they show up in a presentable way?" These are attributes that someone has either sought to embody over decades of living or not.

Arshad said that the second aspect of hiring someone is whether they have the appropriate know-how. Simply put, he looks to see if a candidate has experience that meshes with the requirements for the job at hand. I have heard this basis for hiring people before. On the other hand, it's not that uncommon to hire someone based first on who they are, how they manifest their presence, and then finally look to their professional background. Skill sets can be easily taught; things like presence and communication are harder to train someone in.

One of the things I admire about Arshad is that he has mastered one particular aspect of artfulness: he knows how to put the right people in the right positions. We serve together on the board of an alumni association, and I am always tickled to see who he recommends for any given position. His reasons for choosing people are always sound, so it is hard to argue with him. Because his logic is genuine, he can place people where they ought to be placed and it works out well.

This aspect of artfulness is sometimes referred to as arranging your kingdom. Imagine your life as a kingdom, with you as the monarch. Knowing you cannot do everything or be everywhere, you need to appoint certain people as ministers, others as generals, others as educators, and so on, so that everyone has their rightful place in the kingdom based on their unique abilities.

In the same way, you can view your life with that attitude

of discernment. You can contemplate who you would appoint as ministers—people you trust who can advise you in all matters of your life. Perhaps they are good friends, or siblings, or people you admire at work. Who would play the role of general, protecting you and looking out for you when you need it? These are the people in your life who are unwaveringly there for you when the chips are down. You can build your whole life out in this manner, artfully discerning who should play what role in order for everything to work seamlessly.

In her book *Bossypants*, Tina Fey made the point, "In most cases being a good boss means hiring talented people and then getting out of their way."[1] Artfulness is based in acknowledging the qualities of others and empowering them in ways that make sense for them. Once you select your ministers, generals, and so on, let them serve in that role and trust your decision to empower them. Give them the space to work on your behalf.

Being artful includes consideration of others. The artful leader cares about the people they are leading and wants to know them intimately. I have always been impressed when I hear Arshad on the phone with his employees. He knows so much about them!

Chögyam Trungpa Rinpoche once said that an artful leader cares about all of the details of people's lives, from the type of clothing they wear to how they advance professionally. While I do not know if Arshad keeps an Excel list of each employee's sock choices, I know he has deep regard for the people he works with, and, as a result, they have deep respect for him. Within that context they manifest as the right people for the right position.

TIMING, SPACE, AND COMMUNICATION

Timing is an important element of being artful. If you want your work to flow seamlessly, you need to know when to act and when to give space to a situation. You can set up your day to maximize your time and spend it with coworkers with whom you know you can accomplish a great deal. Alternatively, you can take some time to review your work environment and ask yourself, "What is the most skillful instant to pitch a new idea?" If you just scored a big client, maybe now is a good time to ask for a raise or promotion. When you are present and see your work situation clearly, you will know the best timing for any given act.

An artful leader is one who gives others the space to discover their own wisdom. Chögyam Trungpa Rinpoche often empowered teachers and administrators before they were perfectly trained. It was said that he would give people just enough rope to hang themselves, but he believed in them enough that more often than not, they did just fine. The more we empower our employees in a supportive manner, the more we are able to accomplish together.

Knowing when to engage certain acts can require patience. For example, you may be leading a meeting and a conflict arises. Being artful in this situation might require you to pause the meeting, acknowledge the conflict, and give space and time to it. That may mean you won't accomplish everything on your agenda.

Another aspect of artfulness is knowing when not to act at all. If your energy is fading or you are feeling particularly riled, that is not the time to engage in conflict head-on. Being artful here might mean excusing yourself for a long walk or making yourself a cup of tea.

To return to benevolence, it won't help your cause to leap in and bulldoze over others. In *Hagakure* it says, "Being superior to others is nothing other than having people talk about your affairs and listening to their opinions."[2] We can be our best selves when we actually listen to others and take their opinions into account. The more space you give other people to discover their wisdom—even if that messes with your preconceived notions of what ought to be happening—the more they will come to trust and respect you.

One final aspect of working in an artful manner is that you

know the best way to communicate with others. The artful leader's consideration for others goes beyond just knowing details about their lives; it involves thinking through exactly what each person needs to know and how best to convey that information.

Anyone who has been in a leadership position knows the importance of clear communication. For example, there are some people, like your board of directors, who will need in-depth financial information communicated to them in order to do their job properly. The administrative assistant down the hall may not need all of that information; he only needs to know that cash flow is normal and he will continue to receive his paycheck on time. When you mentally map out your organization you can think about who needs what kind of communication and how they would best be able to hear it.

One of my best friends, Alex, passed away in 2012. He was twenty-nine years old when he unexpectedly collapsed at work. My friend Sean, who worked in the same organization, found out about it right away. He had the difficult task of calling me and breaking the news.

He did a great job of it, which I realize is a weird thing to say about such terrible news. He was direct and clear, and he shared his own pain and heartbreak on the phone with me. After Sean got off the phone, he left work, got in a cab, and came to see me. He knew I would be a wreck and spent the day telling me all of the best things he could possibly say in such circumstances.

His artful communication inspired me to strive to be as giving and precise in my speech that day as well. I realized that, in today's world, it was only a matter of time before people began finding out about this news through Facebook and other electronic means. That would be very poor communication.

At Alex's mother's request, I began calling other friends and telling them, as directly as I could, about Alex's passing. I must have told eight or more people that day. I asked many of them to tell other people I knew they were close with. I just couldn't stand the idea of anyone finding out in a way that would cause them more pain than the news alone, and it seemed like the best way to do that was to let them hear the news from a familiar voice.

Even at that terrible time, I was able to feel the smallest bit of warmth because I felt like I was already beginning to honor Alex's memory by communicating this news in an artful way. It made me feel a small bit better to help in this manner, and it helped others to hear it from a close friend of his. Artful communication is a form of compassion. We feel good engaging in it, and it is a way to share our heart clearly with other people. In difficult times, it helps us and helps others feel respected.

We can't rule our work or our life situation single-handedly. We need to rely on people. A skillful leader sees the unique qualities in others and places them in positions that allow them to shine and feel empowered, while bettering the situation at hand. Through artfully handling our timing and communication, we learn to make our life function like a well-oiled machine. We become powerful, operating seamlessly in our work in a way that provides comfort to others and benefit to all.

18 / REJOICING, OR IT'S OKAY TO PARTY

Birthdays was the worst days; now we sip champagne when we thirsty.

—*Notorious B.I.G.*

The final quality of the Six Ways of Ruling is rejoicing. While it sounds simple enough, many of us don't take the time to celebrate our lives as fully as we should. We have a knack for dwelling on all the upsets that come our way, complaining about our inconveniences, instead of celebrating everything that we have going for us.

The quote from the rap artist Notorious B.I.G. illustrates the concept of rejoicing well. Having come from poverty, he notes that when he was growing up and birthdays would roll around, he would always be disappointed. Having made something of himself career-wise and accumulated great wealth, he now has the luxury of sipping on champagne whenever he wants. He is able to rejoice in his good fortune, likely because his present lifestyle contrasts so starkly with his previous one.

Even if you haven't gone from poverty to affluence, you can rejoice in everything you have in your life. You can celebrate the fact that you have family members who love you, or friends who care for you and support you in your endeavors, or a partner who cherishes you. You most likely have a roof over your head and the ability to feed yourself on a regular basis, which is not the case for many people throughout the world. You have the opportunity to practice meditation and become familiar with your own mind, which can free you from mental anguish. All of these things are worthy of celebration.

In fact, it is foolish that we waste so much time complaining about what we do not have instead of rejoicing in our good fortune. Even if you have had a really rough go of things lately—maybe you've been unemployed or are feeling unappreciated at work—you can still rejoice the various positive elements of your life and recognize the small occasions for rejoicing that take place throughout your day.

EXERCISE FOR REJOICING

This is the power of rejoicing: at any given moment we are able to look at what we have going on in our life and celebrate something. My friend Lucy is a teacher and told me of a helpful practice that she employs at the end of each school year: She sits down to reflect on the previous nine months and makes a list of everything that she is proud of that occurred during that time. There might be major accomplishments, like teaching someone with a learning disability to read after years of struggle, or seemingly lesser things, like having the courage to confront a parent about bullying other teachers.

We can all engage in this type of rejoicing on a monthly, weekly, or even daily basis. You can take a moment at night, after brushing your teeth, just to sit down on your bed and meditate on the question *What have I done today that I can be proud of?*

You can take a paper and pen and jot down whatever comes up in your mind (this isn't shamatha meditation—you don't need to label anything *thinking*). When your mind does wander, though, come back to that question of what you have accomplished.

After you feel like you have exhausted the question, put the paper down and read through your list. Refrain from judgmental thinking, such as "Yesterday's list was longer" or "Is that really worth being proud about?" Just read through the list. After reviewing what you wrote, raise your gaze and relax with whatever emotion may be present. That is rejoicing.

Your World Is Magic

It's actually possible to celebrate whether or not we have something specific to celebrate. With the view that everyone and everything we encounter is rooted in basic goodness, we can find magic in any situation.

You can rejoice that you are driving down the street and your favorite song has come on the radio. You can rejoice that a cute puppy interrupts his walk to come say hello to you. You can even rejoice in being yelled at by your spouse, if you hold the view that you are both basically good and thus there is inherent magic in that interaction.

Along those lines, if someone does something that upsets you, you can still rejoice. You can celebrate that this individual is giving you a chance to work through your own neurosis, or that they are offering you a chance to practice compassion. You can recall the mind-training slogan discussed earlier: "Be grateful to everyone." If we encounter obstacles in our home or work life, they should be celebrated; they remind us of everything we already have within and around us. We can be grateful for their existence and rejoice that we can practice meditative mind at all.

Often when I visit my teacher, Sakyong Mipham Rinpoche, in his personal space, I feel like I just walked into a party. Because he has mastered the Six Ways of Ruling, whenever I see him I am confident that I will have an experience of my own basic goodness, that our conversations will be logical and genuine, and that we will discuss things in an artful and fearless manner. In that environment, celebration organically occurs.

No matter where he is, the physical environment always has an air of festivity. Part of his magic is that his presence alone inspires you to employ these six techniques of leadership so you can create this same feeling of celebration in your own life. When you walk out of a meeting with the Sakyong, you are sad to leave the party but are inspired to follow in his footsteps and create the conditions for rejoicing in your own day-to-day existence.

One of the reasons I find the Sakyong so inspiring is that he carries the weight of the world on his shoulders but always manages to smile and exhibits an incredible sense of humor. He is recognized as the reincarnation of Mipham the Great and holds many responsibilities for monasteries in Tibet and India. And as the spiritual head of the Shambhala Buddhist lineage, he has students all over the Western world looking to him for advice and guidance.

Early on in my path of leadership, I remember asking him if he ever felt lonely as he traveled around the world. Everywhere he goes, people want something from him, and I assumed they rarely would take the time to ask how he was doing or inquire about his many projects. "No," he said, "I don't get lonely." He went on to tell me about his experience traveling and the staff that supports him, and in the course of our conversation I figured out that a spiritual teacher like him doesn't experience loneliness in the same way you or I might.

He is a normal human being, and I believe emotions like loneliness do arise for him. For someone like him, loneliness and other feelings might come up, but I get the sense that he does not let them get their hooks into him like you or I do. He has come to realize the ephemeral quality of these emotions and lets them roll down his back. Because he is not easily hooked by these strong emotions, he is able to come back to the present moment and rejoice in it. He is able to smile and be playful, even with incredible pressure coming at him from all sides.

This ability to rejoice in the midst of great pressure is one of the things that make the Sakyong an incredible leader. Often leaders think they have to hold it all together and become very uptight, even if they don't mean to be. But a good leader is not swayed from the view of basic goodness and knows that it's okay to party.

CELEBRATION

Rejoicing is an important part of the Shambhala Buddhist tradition. When I served as the director of the Boston Shambhala Center, one day I was taking out the trash and stopped to say hello to our neighbors at the auto-body shop next door. One of the mechanics joked that he saw that we had been meditating a great deal lately. "Really," I asked, "how can you tell?" He replied, "We can always tell when a lot of people have been meditating: the dumpster is full of sake bottles."

I was embarrassed, but I ended up reflecting on all the meditation intensives we had hosted that month. The people who had come to the Shambhala Center for these programs had done something pretty uncanny in today's world: they had taken a weekend to meditate for eight to ten hours a day instead of seeing movies, going to barbeques, or hanging out with friends. They had cleared that time to better themselves through the practice of meditation, which is something pretty phenomenal and worth celebrating.

At the end of the intensives, we would gather together and raise a toast in honor of one another, our shared experience, and the people who led the program. Not everyone would drink, of course, but some people would. Rejoicing seemed to be a natural part of the experience. It went hand in hand with exerting ourselves in an endeavor meant to better ourselves and others. People weren't looking to get wasted at these events, but they did enjoy having a drink while taking pride in their experience.

The rough equivalent for that in many organizations is a regular happy hour. People on the same team go out for drinks together and celebrate one another's company, recently completed projects, and won-over clients. I have attended a number of happy hours, both for companies I have worked for and those held for friends' or partners' companies.

A good happy hour seems to be marked by appreciating one another freely, outside of the confines of the habitual work dynamic. A bad happy hour seems to be marked by a perpetuation of the worst aspects of office behavior, including gossip and slander. Particularly when alcohol is tossed into the mix, it is hard to get people to stay in the zone of appreciation and not slip into complaining about the same old garbage.

Whenever I am in a situation like that, I remember the words of the Sakyong: "Celebration is an attitude." Celebration is not empty sake bottles or happy-hour Budweisers. It is an attitude of appreciating our life as it is. That is the example the Sakyong sets: if we are able to be aware of the present moment, celebration comes naturally. We don't have to modify or change anything; we are basically good, our coworkers are basically good, and we can enjoy one another's presence as a result.

Rejoicing is a direct outcome of combining the previous five methods of leadership. When you are benevolent to others, are true to your own goodness, can genuinely point out the logic in a given situation, are fearless in presenting that goodness and logic, and are artful in your execution, a great deal can be accomplished. When that happens, it's only natural to party.

You are capable of leading in this way. You have everything you need to live a life that is in line with the Six Ways of Ruling. You may not be "the boss," but you can still be a leader. You can be a postal delivery worker or a bartender or a receptionist but still be a leader. In any given moment you can wake up to a heart of authentic leadership by exhibiting the Six Ways of Ruling.

Even though you may not have actively sought out a leadership role, if you live a life of mindfulness and empathy, you may simply find yourself becoming a leader, as others come to trust you and are magnetized to you. If you exercise these six techniques of leadership, you may find that you are the kind of leader this world needs. Through working with the Six Ways of Ruling, you can benefit this world greatly, and you will be victorious in all your actions.

PART FOUR

VAJRAYANA

Be Awake for Each Moment

19 / DEVELOPING CONFIDENCE

Kid, you had a rough day. Everyone has them. And when
you do—do what I do—you ask yourself: Anybody's life
better because of what I did today? If the answer's yes . . .
then stop your whining. If not, well, do better tomorrow.

—Comic-book character Nick Fury

Determining who you are is a major aspect of the Buddhist
path. Through the exploration of this path, you may discover
that at your core you are basically good. You are innately kind
and wise. You are capable of being present with your work situation and bringing bodhicitta into the office with you every
day. Furthermore, you can employ the Six Ways of Ruling to
serve as a leader in a way that truly benefits those around you.

At its most fundamental level, the Buddhist path involves
examining your natural state, without taking too much stock
in the confusion that swirls around that. It is realizing that you
are infinitely capable and then developing faith in that notion.
If you do not continuously reflect on your basic nature, bringing mindfulness and compassion into the office is pointless.
That is why it is important to return at this point to the key
notion of determining who we are by developing confidence
in our basic goodness.

Developing true confidence in our basic goodness and in

our abilities is the path of the third vehicle of Tibetan Buddhism: the Vajrayana. *Vajrayana* is a Sanskrit term. *Vajra* can be translated as "diamond" or "indestructible"; *yana*, as we know, means "vehicle." This vehicle has the same powerful, brilliant qualities of a diamond; like a diamond, it is considered indestructible. Nothing can demolish it. Why? Because it focuses deeply on the very core of what we are: our inherent wakefulness.

Our wakefulness, this basically good state, can never be destroyed. It can never be misplaced, evaporated, or washed away. Regardless of our ups and downs at work, regardless of whether we are certain we are doing what we want to be doing career-wise, our basic goodness is always available to us. Like a little voice, it whispers the reminder that we don't have to be confused or uncertain; we can experience our goodness and act from that powerful place.

Another term for the Vajrayana is *tantra*. Tantra can refer to the texts, practices, or rituals from the Buddhist and Hindu traditions that analyze reality; the direct translation is "continuity." But tantra is more than specific practices and texts; it is a way of life. It is the path of developing certainty in our goodness.

The continuity aspect is that it is not just when we are meditating that we can experience our wakefulness. It is not just when times are tough and we reach deep within ourselves to contact that generator of wisdom. It can be continuous. The *Oxford English Dictionary* notes that the Sanskrit origin of the word *tantra* is loom, or groundwork. We can access our basic goodness all the time. It is the ground of our very existence and can serve as the loom upon which we weave our life. That is the nature of tantra: when we develop the right skillful means, we can live a life based entirely in the nature of awake.

UPAYA

Thankfully, there are teachings for developing these methods, or *upaya*, a Sanskrit term that can be translated as "expedient or skillful means." When we have developed prajna and see reality as it actually is, as opposed to how we might want it to be, we spontaneously know how to act in a way that is skillful and helpful. When we employ upaya, we are acting in accord with reality, as opposed to fighting it. We are opening more to our natural state, a state of being awake.

It is said that the Buddha taught the Vajrayana teachings during his lifetime but asked that they remain secret. They were not written down for several generations. Instead, they were passed along from a teacher to a select group of students, some of whom would become teachers themselves and pass along the oral lineage to their students. These lineages of ritual and skillful means would help practitioners develop full confidence in their awake nature during one lifetime. Hence, it was a path known for its expediency.

When the Buddha became enlightened, it is said that the first thing he did upon getting up from that experience was walk to the nearby river and throw in his begging bowl. The bowl skipped upstream, against the current, instead of doing what it would normally do, which is float downstream.

I imagine this as something of an "uh-oh" moment for the Buddha. He knew that this symbolic gesture meant that everything he would then be teaching would be considered against the stream of societal norms. His teachings would be countercultural.

In today's world, engaging in the process of slowing down and discovering that you aren't, in fact, basically struggling and pitiful but are instead good and worthy is countercultural. We are taught from a young age that we are not good enough, smart enough, or worthy of anything unless we can earn enough money to buy it.

This is a fundamental obstacle to realizing our true potential. If we cannot work through this obstacle with a variety of skillful means, then we will spend our lives wallowing in our own suffering and uncertainty. We will never have the confidence to make the decisions we need to make in life and will rely on the latest boss, partner, or gadget to make them for us. If we long to be our most authentic self, then we need to overcome this obstacle and develop true confidence in our own goodness and our unique abilities.

EXERCISE IN EXAMINING LABELS

One aspect of developing confidence in your basic nature is realizing that you are not your obstacles. A large obstacle such as "I'm not good enough" or "I will never be able to do what I actually want to do" can feel crippling. If you let it, it will become a major part of the identity you create for yourself and can prevent you from realizing who you actually could be.

We create identities for ourselves all the time. Many of these can limit us from our true potential, so it is best to examine them and see our way through them to deepening our understanding of our basic state. To start this exercise, grab a pen and a piece of paper. Take a moment to sit upright, in something resembling your meditation posture. Place your attention on your breath, sitting shamatha for a minute or two.

Then, sit with the question *What labels do I place on myself?* These labels could be words like *sister, son,* or *good friend* or qualities like *kind person* or *funny guy.* Maybe words come up that are work related, including your role or your position in relation to other people in your company: *retail associate, boss,* or *assistant.* Whatever comes up, note it on your paper.

After a few minutes, put down your pen and return to shamatha. Sit for another minute or two to conclude your session. Afterwards, turn your attention to the list you created. Are you surprised by some of the labels you place on yourself? The order in which they came up? Or does that list make perfect sense to you?

Finally, ask yourself a few questions. "Is this list me?" Contemplate whether that list defines who you are. If not, what is missing? Conclude by asking yourself, "Is everything on this list the same as it was five years ago? Will this list be the same five years from now?" Notice whatever feelings arise during this process.

This exercise points out just how many labels we place on ourselves. We define ourselves in relation to other people, in relation to our subjective sense of who we are or long to be, and by what we do in or out of work. We don't often define ourselves as "basically wise" or "innately good."

These labels change constantly. If you are a mother who loses her child, does that make you no longer a mother? If you snap at someone when you are in a bad mood, does that negate the fact that you are generally a nice person?

A core belief in the Buddhist tradition is *anatman*, a Sanskrit term that translates as "not-self." It is the idea that you are not the set, solid being that you think you are. You are a fluid, constantly evolving and changing person who can play a variety of roles and embody a variety of qualities over time. You are not a permanent expression of the labels you put on yourself but more of a fluid entity that shifts in accordance with what comes up in your life.

So when you are faced with obstacles, you can remember that you are not the labels you put on yourself. You do not need to be defined by your obstacles. You can transcend them. You can go beyond your normal understanding of who you think you are and, when in touch with your basic goodness, you can overcome anything as a result. These are the times when we develop true faith in our own abilities.

WORKING SKILLFULLY WITH OBSTACLES

How we respond to obstacles is what actually defines us. We can transcend obstacles and upheavals through the skillful means, the upaya, of facing situations head on. We can transmute obstacles into opportunities for growth if we can learn to respond to them straightforwardly.

Chögyam Trungpa Rinpoche once said "You can appreciate your life, even if it is an imperfect situation." The reason we can appreciate it is that we can look to all of the imperfect aspects of our life as opportunities to learn more about ourselves and our world. Instead of acting out in a habitual manner, we can train ourselves in new ways of relating to our world, ways that put us more in touch with our basic nature of awake.

If we recognize obstacles as merely part of the display of our world, then we realize we don't have to take them—or ourselves—so seriously. You are not this heavy, solid thing but a vast conglomeration of knowledge and experience that is ever-changing. Similarly, when you face an obstacle, you should think of it in the same impermanent, fluid way.

People deal with all sorts of obstacles at work. There is the fear of failure, plus confrontations with mindless bureaucracy, with other people's egos, with your own ego, with unethical practices, with incompetence, and a wide variety of issues related to race, gender, and sexual orientation which no HR manual will ever be able to cover in full.

At the beginning of this chapter, the comic-book character Nick Fury offers us some advice for when we encounter obstacles or have a rough day. The first thing to remember is that you are not alone. Every single person who has held a job or sat on a meditation cushion has encountered obstacles. Every single one. We can take comfort in the fact that we are not the only ones experiencing this particular form of suffering.

However, we need to overcome the obstacle. If you become paralyzed by a fear of failure, or by becoming lost in a bureaucracy, then you are letting yourself be defined by that paralysis. You are only suffocating yourself. You are, in some sense, losing yourself by solidifying your world in a way that paints it as unworkable.

Everything is workable. If you have confidence in the fact that you are basically good—that this is the deepest reality about who you are—then every situation you encounter becomes an opportunity to be of benefit to yourself and others. Every situation gives you a chance to develop faith in your own abilities.

With that view, you can acknowledge the obstacles and upheavals that come your way, but you do not need to let them weigh you down. Just as when a strong emotion comes up on the meditation cushion, we can gently acknowledge it as an obstacle but then come back to whatever it is that is going on in the present moment.

The more you align yourself with the present moment, the more you will be able to practice upaya, the skillful or expedient means that spontaneously arise when you are grounded in seeing the reality of a situation. When you do that you can act from the standpoint of your basic goodness, allowing your obstacle to serve as a jumping-off point for further continuity of your basic state of awake. The more you tap into that state and develop confidence in it, the more you will be able to engage your livelihood and life in a way that you feel good about. You can then reflect on whether anyone else's life is better because of your skillful means. If the answer is yes, then stop complaining about obstacles. If the answer is no, tomorrow is a new day.

20 / IT'S HARD OUT HERE FOR A PIMP

Right Livelihood Revisited

Son, appearances are not the issue.
Rather, attachment to them is.
So Naropa, cut attachment.

—*Tilopa*[1]

Tilopa is the founding father of the Kagyu school of Tibetan Buddhism. I feel a certain family pride in this lineage. Raised by parents who studied extensively with the Kagyu master Chögyam Trungpa Rinpoche, I was brought up with tales of the great Kagyu forefathers. However, many of these lineage holders were eccentric individuals, with life stories to match. The common thread through all of them is that they were normal people, like you and me, who through the practice of meditation developed certainty in their awakened state and proved to be of great use to our world.

Tilopa may be one of the more out-there members of this family tree. He was born into the Brahmin caste in India in 988 and lived until 1069. In his early years, he went to school and became an excellent scholar. It is said that when he was twenty, he was visited by a *dakini* who invited him to pursue the dharma more diligently.

The term *dakini* can be translated directly from Sanskrit as "sky dancer" or "sky walker." There is a great deal to say about the Buddhist concept of the dakini, but a succinct way to explain these beings is that they are considered the female embodiment of enlightened energy. Acharya Judith Simmer-Brown, who wrote an excellent book on this topic, has pointed out that a dakini might manifest as a meditational deity upon whom we can focus to inspire qualities within us or as a wrathful protector of the teachings.[2] There are stories of dakinis as embodiments of wisdom energy and stories of dakinis as tantric female practitioners of the dharma.

The dakinis are said to have played a major role in Tilopa's spiritual development. We know he studied with renowned teachers, including Nagarjuna and Matangi, and under their instruction proved adept at meditative discipline. However, he is said to have achieved wisdom mind through his interactions with the sky dancers. Regardless of the influence of his human teachers versus that of the dakinis, we know he was inspired to go into a cave and meditate for twelve years.

Believe it or not, we're not at the eccentric part yet. After attaining vast mastery over his own mind, Tilopa was approached by his teacher Matangi, who told him to go back into the world. Because Tilopa came from a royal background, he still carried some pride and arrogance, which were inhibiting his spiritual progress.

Matangi's solution was for Tilopa to go to Bengal and work as the assistant to a prostitute named Bharima. This is where we get even more unconventional. During the day Tilopa worked for Bharima pounding sesame seed into oil. (*Til* is a Sanskrit word meaning "sesame.") He was so well known for this period of his life that, centuries later, we know him as the sesame pounder. That was his day job. At night, Tilopa would solicit customers for Bharima's prostitution business.

It was during this period that Tilopa is said to have achieved complete enlightenment. Taking the simple work of pounding sesame seeds as part of his practice, he pounded the pride and arrogance out of his being. By being a helpful servant to a woman of the night, he learned to be of benefit to everyone he encountered. Through his work, Tilopa realized coemergent wisdom.

This may seem shocking to you. You picked up this book looking for advice on living a spiritual work life, and here I am telling you the story of a famous pimp. However, this famous pimp achieved awakening by taking on humble work, committing fully to it, and making it a part of his spiritual practice.

This is the level of conviction that is taught in the Vajrayana tradition. Tilopa is the forefather of the Kagyu school of Vajrayana teachings, and his wisdom was passed down to his student Naropa, who passed it on to his student Marpa, who passed it on to Milarepa, who passed it on to Gampopa, who passed it on to the Karmapa, who for seventeen incarnations has been the head of the Karma Kagyu school of Tibetan Buddhism.

The Kagyu masters' teachings on realization continue to the present day. The commitment and example of Tilopa is, in that sense, not old news at all. It is a fresh example of how we can switch our view of work so that everything we encounter is considered a part of our path.

Tilopa went on to teach widely. As soon as he achieved awakening, people recognized it. He was radiant. His prostitute friend, Bharima, came forward and felt remorse for treating such a high spiritual being with such disregard. However, within minutes it is said that she too achieved awakening. Having spent so much time in the presence of someone who exhibited the qualities of bodhicitta and awakened mind, she was ripe for her own spiritual development.

THREE LESSONS FROM TILOPA'S STORY

There are three morals I would like to pull from the story of Tilopa. The first is his commitment to his practice. You may not have the time to head into a cave to meditate for twelve years. However, an interesting aspect of Tilopa's story is that he did not achieve complete enlightenment during that period. He did something that you and I can do: he pinpointed the aspects of himself that he needed to work on, and chipped away at his negative habitual patterns through working a job that he may not necessarily have loved.

Matangi did not tell Tilopa to go be a teacher or to hole up in a monastery somewhere. He told Tilopa to go do relatively low-class, perhaps even humiliating work. From a conventional point of view, that might sound horrible. From the point of view of someone looking to hammer out arrogance, that is a ripe opportunity for purifying his mind.

That leads us to the second moral: Tilopa went to work as a pimp for a specific reason at a specific time in a specific place. He didn't go into that line of work because he thought it would be fun. It was the appropriate upaya, or skillful means, for him to work through his neurotic hang-ups. In a similar vein, we can pinpoint the work that will help us develop in a spiritual capacity.

While traveling in Prague, I was out to dinner one evening and overheard the gentleman at the next table speaking English. After a few days of not encountering many English speakers, I felt emboldened to ask him where he was from. He was a British expat who had made Prague his home for a number of years. As we got to talking, I inquired about his line of work.

"I run an international dating service," he responded. I remarked that in the United States these days there are many Web sites that serve as dating services, and that it seemed like a ripe industry. As our conversation progressed, it became apparent that he did something a little bit different from match.com. He screened Western European and American men and matched them with Eastern European ladies. "In other words," I asked, "you run a foreign bride agency?"

My dining companion concurred. He said he actually felt quite good about being able to provide this service and introduce people who otherwise would never have the chance to meet. Soon he was joined by a beautiful woman whom he clearly was meeting for the first time. I excused myself from our conversation, but quickly caught on that this woman was auditioning to be one of the potential brides for his service. At the end of the night, the two of them left hand in hand. As he walked out the door, this fellow shot me a knowing wink.

I mention this story because it feels completely different from Tilopa's tale. This man struck me as, frankly, a sleazy fellow who seemed to be profiting from the power dynamic between rich men and good-looking women who were desperate to escape their country of origin. While I may be projecting a bit too far here, I also got the impression that he slept with some of these women as part of their screening process. The encounter left me with a mixture of shock, disbelief, and the chills.

My dining companion is no Tilopa. Tilopa's motivation was spiritual awakening. Though his work is illegal in today's world, it led him and others to enlightenment. This mail-order bride executive seemed entirely motivated by sex and money. He seemed to be deceiving himself that he was arranging for true love, when in fact he did not really know what happened to these women after they left the Czech Republic.

In other words, we should not consider Tilopa's story as a free pass to do whatever we want for our occupation and call it right livelihood. Instead, we need to consider our livelihood from the perspective of how it can help us to hammer away at our neurosis, instead of encourage it.

If and only if we can cut through our attachment to appearances, as Tilopa advised Naropa, then we can engage in almost any line of work. However, knowing why we're doing the work, and holding the motivation that part of the why is that we are working with our neurotic mind, is important.

To return to the first moral of Tilopa's story, we should commit ourselves to waking up through our work, treating it as a spacious meditation hall in which our neurosis can exhaust itself. With the view that our office is a practice ground, we are truly joining our spiritual and work lives in a Vajrayana manner. All obstacles that arise are relished, as they are part of our spiritual endeavor.

The third moral of the story of Tilopa, from my personal point of view, is that we may be surprised by the effect this level of commitment has on others. Sure, pounding sesame seeds day in and day out might help pound your own arrogance out of you, but it turns out that when you're done pounding the seeds and are less arrogant, you are treating people in a kinder, saner way.

Because you are living a spiritual life while you're on the clock, other people are picking up on your energy and may start acting in a similar manner, whether they are aware of it or not. On a purely energetic level, you are shifting the nature of your work environment through your commitment to practice.

In the case of Bharima, I doubt she realized that she was practicing the dharma in any shape or form. She was going about her business sleeping with people for money. Yet by having Tilopa, a deeply spiritual person, by her side day after day, month after month, she was naturally ripened to the point where she had inadvertently become a spiritual person.

Compared to Bharima, Jane the annoying nag in accounting probably seems overripe for mindfulness and compassion teachings. You may not feel comfortable talking to Jane about your meditation practice, and that's okay.

Simply by committing to your practice in a manner akin to Tilopa, you may end up exhibiting the qualities that come with being present and acting from bodhicitta. Your spiritual life will naturally pervade the work environment, and Jane may be affected by that. If Bharima can achieve enlightenment primarily from hanging out with Tilopa, I am guessing Jane probably has a shot at becoming kinder just by hanging out around you.

THE SIX WORDS OF ADVICE

One of the teachings that Tilopa gave to his student Naropa is known as the "Six Words of Advice." It is called that because the text in Tibetan is made up of only six words. They are excellent instructions on the mahamudra teachings of Tibetan Buddhism, which, from the traditional view of *ultimate* truth, point to the truth of *shunyata,* or the emptiness of all phenomena. But from the corresponding and complementary view of *relative* truth, they can be wonderfully applicable to life in general as well. The author and Tibetan Buddhist teacher Ken McLeod has translated these six words as follows:

> Don't recall.
> Don't imagine.
> Don't think.
> Don't examine.
> Don't control.
> Rest.

He has also provided a slightly longer translation as an aid in understanding this very short text:

> Let go of what has passed.
> Let go of what may come.
> Let go of what is happening now.
> Don't try to figure anything out.
> Don't try to make anything happen.
> Relax, right now, and rest.[3]

Don't recall, or Let go of what has passed.

Here Tilopa exhorts us to let go of the past, avoiding memories of what once was. For example, you may have a friend who loves to spend time talking about how great his old job was compared to his current position. The hours were better, the year-end bonuses larger, his coworkers more fun to hang out with. Yet if he took a fraction of the time he spends complaining and applied it to a job search, he might find a situation that is more in line with what he wants to do.

Dwelling in what has already passed is like living in a cinema. You may get some sort of satisfaction from the experience, but eventually the lights come up and you return to a reality that differs from the one you had been enjoying.

We don't need to wallow in the memories of when work was more fun or when we had a boss who treated us better. We can let all of that go.

Don't imagine, or Let go of what may come.

Similarly, there is no need to project what may happen tomorrow or the next day. We can let go of what may or may not happen in the future. We don't need to daydream about promotions or raises that may or may not come. There is no sense in imagining what might happen, as we could spend days if not months lost in thoughts about things that may never occur.

If your friend gave up complaining about the past and instead spent his life talking about how good he would be at imaginary jobs, he would still be dissatisfied. He would not be trying to find contentment in his present situation or looking for a way to be happy at a different position. He would just be living in a fantasy world, not helping himself or anyone else.

Don't think, or Let go of what is happening now.

Don't fixate on what is going on right now, overanalyzing it to no end. Your friend could sit there and list ad nauseam exactly what is wrong with corporate, why his goals are not attainable, and who is going to suffer from these unrealistic expectations. He has spent a lot of time thinking about the situation but not doing anything about it. The instruction here would be for him to let go of what he thinks is happening, as well as of his fixed views about it. When we are in similar positions we should also not fixate on what we perceive is happening.

Don't examine, or Don't try to figure anything out.

As soon as you bring your analytical mind to trying to slice into a topic, even if it is the present moment, you are missing the point. Don't feel that you need to intellectualize anything.

Instead of getting lost in his own head, your friend could drop the idea that he has to figure out exactly what is going on. We, too, might in similar situations want to figure it all out. Don't give in to that habitual urge.

Don't control, or Don't try to make anything happen.

This one may be my favorite. In this moment, give up the idea that you have to control anything at all. You might encourage your friend to give up the notion that he has to create something or fix something or get something right.

Rest, or Relax, right now, and rest.

After a series of instructions about what we should not do, Tilopa finally gives us something to do, which is not do anything. We are advised not to let our mind wander into the past or the future. That leaves us with the present moment—what is going on right now. In the present moment we should not think too much about what's going on. We should not try to fix anything, or make anything happen, or figure out what anything means.

We should just relax and rest with right now. We should just be available to the present moment, as it is. That is the instruction that Tilopa is trying to hammer into our heads. We should always relax. In that sense, we are never off duty. We can always do this, day and night. We can always rest our mind in this very moment. When we do, we follow in the footsteps of Tilopa and can utilize our work as the fodder for awakening.

21 / LET GO OF MY EGO

The teachings are always available, like a radio signal in
the air. But a student needs to learn how to tune into that
signal, and how to stay tuned in.

—*Sakyong Mipham Rinpoche*

Giving up is a loaded term in our Western world. It denotes failure. It implies that you tried to do something, experienced
obstacles, and decided that thing was not worth doing. This
notion of giving up is the polar opposite of the Buddhist way of
thinking about it.

In the Buddhist context, *giving up* means that you are surrendering everything that is holding you back from experiencing reality in a direct and pure manner. Surrendering is viewed
as positive. We are surrendering everything that stops us from
being available to the teachings of the Buddha. We are giving
up anything that might block the radio signal of the dharma.

Previously we discussed giving up our fixed notions of the
way things should be, as well as practicing generosity in offering material goods, comfort, time, and energy as a means to
open up our heart further. In the Vajrayana context, giving up is
about letting go of every set self-image we project onto ourselves and all preconceived notions of our work and our world,
by emptying ourselves of our own personal garbage.

In terms of applying these teachings to our work situation, we need to give up territory. The strongest and most efficient leaders I know are the ones who are artful enough to drop their own sense of what needs to happen and empower other people to make things run smoothly. They do not need to claim work as their own. They have no attachment to status or title; they are simply willing to do what it takes to get the work done.

In order to give up territory, you need to not take things so personally. If you are heading up one project and get called away for another, you don't need to give into fear-based thinking that everything will fall apart without you. You can trust in the situation, in the wisdom of your peers, and step away graciously. That is giving up territory, offering yourself in a helpful manner, without clinging to "my project" or "my team." It is opening up to the fluid and changing nature of reality, and checking "me" at the door.

In the Vajrayana tradition, the method for giving up territory is surrendering ego. I am reminded of those commercials for Eggo waffles back in the eighties: family members would fight over who would get to eat the precious toaster-waffle, with a tug-of-war over a single waffle and the disputants yelling: "Leggo my Eggo!"

Modifying this commercial a bit, we should habituate ourselves to fight to let go of our ego. We should be diligent in considering how our preconceived notions of self and other hold us back from experiencing the world as it is. We can explore the notions that the more we let go of "me" and "what I need to be happy," the more we will be available to the way things are. When we are purely available to our world, we can experience it as sacred.

THE GURU

An important aspect of the Vajrayana path is making yourself available to a spiritual teacher, often referred to as a guru. Guru is a Sanskrit term which can be translated as "teacher" or "master." A true guru is an individual who has fully let go of their ego, embraced a set of teachings, and embodies those teachings in a real and living manner. There is nothing inauthentic about a guru of this nature.

However, there are people today who do not empty themselves of their ego and decide that their self-developed trip is the wisdom that this world needs. Identifying themselves as superspiritual beings, they arrogantly propagate their own point of view. If they are charismatic enough, they might even attract followers.

Often these self-styled teachers become hypocritical and end up treading on their own teachings; for example, they may preach abstinence while sleeping with their own students. Over time, people become hip to their hypocrisy and the whole affair falls apart. The existence of such people does not mean that we should rule out working with a guru, but that we should be wary of whom we choose as a teacher.

I have seen two patterns when it comes to new practitioners and seeking a guru. Some people walk in the door of a meditation center and, after getting bored with shamatha instruction, wish to see the head teacher. "Surely if I have a guru, my meditation practice will be more interesting!" they think. The desire for a teacher, in this case, is often fueled by boredom or frustration with meditation practice.

Sakyong Mipham Rinpoche has pointed out that when we hit the roadblock of boredom on the meditation cushion, we should not look to other factors to make us less bored. If you are sitting there with your own mind, then it is only you that is boring. Finding a more experienced teacher is not going to make your mind more fascinating.

When people say they are ready to take on a guru, I like to poke at their logic a little bit. Often a new student who wants a guru doesn't understand that relationship very well. They just want someone who will give them personalized instructions, which is a form of trying to feel very special. It is ego promotion instead of neurosis deflation.

These individuals may think they are above the traditional practices that have addressed students' neurosis over thousands of years. They want someone who will do their spiritual work for them, analyzing their habitual patterns so that they are no longer burdened with that task. That is a fixed perspective of what the relationship should look like, one that ought to be given up.

The second way I have seen new practitioners approach the topic of seeking a guru is with a kind of horror of the idea of this relationship. This hesitancy strikes me as healthy. Many people base their happiness on external factors, as opposed to connecting with their own awake qualities. When someone who lives a life based in connecting with the quality of awake comes along, you can't help doubting that they are the real deal. You are wary of them at first.

It is said that when approaching a spiritual teacher, a healthy skepticism is desirable. You should test the waters before diving into a teacher-student relationship. Be sure that they are someone genuine who embodies wisdom and doesn't just possess an intellectual understanding of the teachings.

When you do find someone you think is an authentic teacher, you will naturally grow to admire them. Admiration in this case does not involve trying to consume spiritual teachings or win over a teacher by making them like us. Instead, we are sharing in their immense vision for spiritual awakening, and this leaves us inspired to heed their advice. At that point the relationship shifts and the teacher can become helpful in highlighting all the subtle ways we deceive ourselves into buying into passion, aggression, and ignorance.

The teacher-student relationship is based in us grinding away our inauthentic points. It is like we are a tough boulder and the teacher plants little pieces of dynamite at our rough edges. As we heed the advice of a spiritual teacher, our pride, arrogance, pettiness, and so on are blown away. Then we are able to relate to our teacher and the world in a naked and direct way, smoothed over like a precious stone.

OUR LIFE AS TEACHER

Seeking a guru in human form is a traditional aspect of practicing the Vajrayana. However, there are other ways to learn to untangle the complicated ball of yarn that is our ego. Chögyam Trungpa Rinpoche has said, "Surrendering to the 'guru' could mean opening our minds to life situations as well as to an individual teacher."[1]

That is the way many people might want to think of "surrendering to the guru" at the early stages of the path. They may not be ready to leap into a formal relationship with a teacher. It took me many years of examining Sakyong Mipham Rinpoche before one day I spontaneously realized that he was the perfect teacher for me. Do not feel like you have to rush out and grab a guru like you would a new pair of shoes. That line of thinking is materialistic and flies in the face of the Vajrayana teachings.

Instead, you can take Trungpa Rinpoche's advice and look to your own life situations as opportunities for processing your neuroses. Although a teacher can be very helpful, you don't need one to come to terms with the fact that you still have a lot of mental hang-ups. You probably have already discovered that all by yourself.

Instead of relying on others for your inner transformation, you can look at every situation in your life as a chance to explore where you are still hanging on to emotional attachment. You can become diligent about noticing your reactions to everyday occurrences at the office. If you see yourself wallowing in self-pity over being stuck with a bad assignment, take that as an opportunity to give up self-pity. If you see yourself growing anxious about an upcoming deadline, take that as a chance to give up anxiety. Whenever you notice emotions are attaching their hooks to you, gently reach in and pry them out.

Offering

One method of giving up or surrendering is offering yourself entirely to your life situation. There are three aspects of offering in this way: body, speech, and mind. You can offer your body to whatever work situation arises, bringing yourself fully into the center of whatever action is taking place. By diving head first into any project that arises, you are giving of yourself without hesitation. This means surrendering set notions of how long something should take, or whom you do or don't want to work with. You are just giving up to the state of affairs that day.

Giving up your speech means that you are using it to the best of your ability to be helpful to the situation. You know that your speech has tremendous power. Here you offer that power without reservation or concern for yourself. You speak in a manner that appreciates the potency of your circumstances as well as the basic goodness that is inherent in the task at hand.

Finally, you can offer your mind. You can let go of me-based thinking completely. Whatever aspects of your innate wisdom present themselves, you surrender to the group at large, knowing it will be of benefit to the situation. Speaking about offering body, speech, and mind, Chögyam Trungpa Rinpoche said, "In other words, we are giving the giver, so there ceases even to be a gift. It is just letting go." Following Tilopa's "Six Words of Advice," we are letting go, relaxing into the situation by surrendering completely to it.

If you can relax to that extent, if you can truly let go, then you are essentially coughing up your neurosis. You are expunging it from your being, by freeing yourself from letting passion, aggression, and ignorance control you. By offering up all aspects of yourself and your desire for territory or status, you are making room for the dharma. You are making yourself available to tune in to the teachings like a radio signal.

Trungpa Rinpoche has said on this topic, "The greatest gift we can make is to open and expose ourselves." By offering up our ego, we are making ourselves open and exposed. We have cleared room for mindfulness and bodhicitta. We have surrendered so many concepts that there is room for the awakened state to be experienced.

TRUST

There is a level of trust that must be displayed in the Vajrayana. We have to trust our own basic goodness as well as that of other people. Furthermore, we have to switch our allegiance from a dualistic perspective to thinking of the entire world as based in this innate worthiness, this core awake nature. When we realize that the world is already awake, it reveals itself as magical.

That means that every life situation is already sacred and wonderful. Obstacles are not obstacles; with the right perspective, they are already workable situations. In this sense, we aren't transmuting anything other than our point of view.

In order to experience the phenomenal world and our life situation as sacred, we must trust in basic goodness on a large scale. We must train ourselves in surrendering all of our fixed expectations, points of view, and neuroses in order to see the world as it truly is. We have to give up our rough edges in order to clear out the room for bodhicitta and awake mind to manifest within us.

We surrender all of our hang-ups because we would like to communicate with the world without our fixed lenses of me-based thinking. We can tune in to that signal of dharma and stay tuned in. We just need to give up and relax with what is.

AN ON-THE-SPOT PRACTICE FOR GIVING UP

There is a common practice used in improvisational comedy troupes that may prove helpful in learning how to surrender into life's situations. It is known as the "yes and" rule. Simply put, it is the idea that in an improv scene, you should never shoot down a situation but instead support it, offering yourself to it.

If someone walks into your scene and asks, "Why are you dressed up as a squirrel?" you can't reply, "I'm not a squirrel, I'm a doctor!" That is closing yourself off from the scene, undercutting the other person, and taking things down a negative road.

Instead, you have to surrender to the situation. You can say something like, "What do you mean? It's Squirrel Tuesday at the office. Didn't you know?" All of a sudden you agreed with your partner and added information to the scene. You are not just dressed as a squirrel; it's Squirrel Tuesday! You may not have initially intended to be a squirrel in that scene, but you can now resign yourself to being a squirrel.

This way of saying yes is a form of surrender. You are giving yourself entirely to something—it could be an improv scene, a new account, or a new career path. You leap in and say yes and add whatever value you can to the scenario.

You are saying yes to reality, to the phenomenal world, and frankly this feels good. This form of surrender may be scary at first, but if we want to open ourselves up to the world around us and succeed in our endeavors, this "yes and" approach is worth pursuing. Through the process of surrender, we open ourselves up to the phenomenal world and move toward realizing the nature of things as they are.

22 / STRIPPERS, LIFE COACHES, AND CULTIVATING AN AUTHENTIC PRESENCE

Having engaged the principles of mindfulness and compassion, at work and through leadership, you may notice that you are becoming a kinder, more genuine human being. That is pretty much the point of this whole exercise in meditation practice. In fact, Chögyam Trungpa Rinpoche has said that the aim of Shambhala Buddhist training is to "become a real person who can help others."[1]

That's it. There is no big secret that will be revealed (but thanks for sticking with the book thus far). We are becoming more awake to our basic nature, our own goodness and worthiness, and thus are able to be helpful to the world at large.

When you start contemplating the Vajrayana path, you may think that something radical will change within you. That's not really the case; you are simply becoming more you. The idea of basic goodness is that more you is exactly what this world needs. When you are your most authentic self, you can serve the world in a powerful way. You can offer the most potent aspects of who you actually are. As we develop conviction in our basic goodness through our work and surrender our neurosis, we become not different but more authentic.

There is a Tibetan term that describes the quality of someone who, through the practice of meditation, has developed an authentic presence: *wangthang,* which can be directly translated as "field of power."

Think of a time when you felt confident in your own skin. A time when you felt completely relaxed being you. You weren't trying to impress anyone or show off. You might have been out with friends or just working away at your desk. Did you have any interesting interactions with other people? Did anyone compliment you on how you looked or strike up a conversation for no real reason? It is distinctly possible that they did.

That is the power of being authentic. When you exhibit wangthang, this authentic presence, people are magnetized to you. It is like you have a gravitational pull that draws coworkers, friends, even strangers into your field of power. They want to be around you because you inspire them to relax and be authentic too.

It is taught that there are outer and inner ways in which authentic presence manifests. From the outer perspective, it is said that if you come to understand cause and effect—karma— you will work to achieve some merit or virtue, and this manifests in your being. When you are living a life that is dignified, it is apparent from your presence. You literally radiate virtue, which is genuinely who you are. People pick up on that and want to work with you, be around you, and soak in that virtue.

The inner form of authentic presence comes from what was discussed in the previous chapter: letting go. You have surrendered your ego and are in tune with reality as it is. You have made yourself available to receive the teachings because you aren't so obsessed with yourself. This process of giving up your neurosis is also virtuous, and it brings inner authentic presence. Because you aren't so wrapped up in your own head, you naturally work more to assist others. Your openness leads you to exhibit this field of power.

These two forms of authentic presence combined lead to a sense of wholesomeness that makes life brilliant and powerful.

This is not the cookie-cutter 1950s version of wholesomeness; it is the idea that we accept and cherish every aspect of who we are. People trust us, and thus we are free to work more diligently to help our company and the world. We can be authentic leaders and offer a sense of command that people are inspired by, because they can feel that power is being wielded effectively and for the good of all.

The more we cultivate virtue and exhibit this authentic presence, the more we can ride the energy of our life. In Shambhala this energy comes directly from the fact that we are manifesting our innate state, our basic goodness. The energy itself is known as windhorse.

WINDHORSE

Windhorse is the translation of the Tibetan word *lungta*. *Lung* means "wind," and *ta* means "horse." It is the idea that at any time we can ride the wind, or energy, of our life, just as we would a horse. We can hop on whatever comes up, good or bad, and ride that energy supported by conviction in our basic goodness.

If you are waiting in a reception room for an important meeting, that is a time you can check in with yourself to manifest windhorse. You can let go of what you think ought to happen in the coming hour. You can touch in with your basic goodness. Having let go and contacted your goodness, you can relax into the energy that comes out of that experience. That is windhorse.

Please note that this is not the formal instruction for the meditation practice of raising windhorse, which should be taught within a retreat format. However, we do not need in-depth instructions to connect with our basic goodness and let the energy from that experience inspire us. That is something that is available to us at any time.

This energy that comes from touching our basic goodness can be whipped up into a wind of delight. When we act from this authentic place, there is no room for doubt. We are not lost in second-guessing our presentation or wondering whether we should be the one taking this meeting. We are just in tune with the environment, which is sacred. We are in touch with our innate wisdom, which is always there waiting to be discovered. We are willing to leap into whatever happens next, fearless and brave. That is how windhorse supports us and how it inspires us to continue to develop our authentic presence.

Exhibiting an unwavering authentic presence is not solely connected to waiting for meetings, of course. You can be a taxi driver rushing around your city or a bartender hustling behind the bar but still maintain this field of power, displaying your upliftedness. In fact, people in those professions see so many customers each day that they have many more opportunities to bring others into the gravitational field of their genuineness, thus motivating others to be authentic too. Wangthang has the same magnetizing effect no matter what you do for work. So long as you are authentic in your occupation, you can do amazing things.

THE LIFE COACH AND THE STRIPPER

I met my friend Hylke—a longtime meditation practitioner, life coach, and consultant—through the Shambhala Center in New York City. He leads transformational workshops throughout the United States, entering major corporations and working with teams to uncover where communication has broken down and redevelop trust among employees.

Hylke is an interesting guy. I can't say exactly how we became friends, but I know I was magnetized to him shortly after meeting him. In retrospect, I realize it must have been because of his overwhelmingly authentic presence. To this day I cannot sit down with him without relaxing into my own genuine state within minutes and discussing matters from that shared perspective. Our conversations are always good ones because he inspires that in me, and I know he inspires it in others as well.

I was joking with a friend about Hylke and how hard it is to casually shoot the shit with someone like that. She told me a story about running into him on the street. He asked her the simplest question: "How are you doing?" Hylke asked it so genuinely that she immediately broke down crying. "I broke up with my boyfriend!" she sobbed. He offered a supportive presence and spoke with her for a few minutes until they had to part ways. Even in this simplest of interactions, Hylke was able to inspire a sincere response from her.

One thing I admire about Hylke is that he is always checking in on his own state of mind. He examines the various labels he places on himself, and when one has firmly plastered itself onto him, he gently peels it off. He has mastered the art of surrendering his neurosis, over and over again.

As a result of his meditation and self-examination, he is genuinely himself. It is always a relief to see him, because that gives me permission to be myself too. It does not matter what activity we do together; because we are able to be our authentic selves, whatever we do is a relaxing experience. That is the beauty of someone who exhibits an authentic presence: they put others at ease and bring them to a calm, relaxed, and genuine state.

I met Caitlin in Portland at an event for my first book. A mutual friend introduced us, and we all went out for drinks afterward at a bar down the road. I felt drawn to Caitlin in the same way I feel drawn to Hylke; within minutes of meeting, we had relaxed into an authentic vibe and thus were able to get to know each other quickly.

Because she was so sincere and present, it came out during our first hour of conversation that she lives a rather unusual lifestyle. In fact, she may be the only polyamorous Buddhist stripper I know. Both her work and her love life are outside my wheelhouse of experience, so I became very curious about them. Since I didn't want to leap to the conclusion that she wasn't genuine in these aspects of her life, over time I engaged her in multiple conversations about how she resolved any philosophical discrepancies between her work and her Buddhist practice.

Interestingly enough, I'm convinced that she is just as genuine at work as she is when we hang out or talk by phone. Caitlin is a dancer, an artist, and a writer, but her paid employment right now is at a strip club in Portland. She goes there a few nights a week, dances, spends time with both men and women, and enjoys their company. She told me that she doesn't drink or abuse drugs at work, nor does she cross any sexual lines with clients. At her core she is a performer, and this is one of the places she performs.

I worry that some readers may think that Caitlin had a horrid childhood or that she is deluding herself in thinking that she can be both a Buddhist and a stripper. To those readers I might reply, "What about Tilopa being a pimp?" To return to what we discussed earlier, the idea of a "good" or "bad" profession is purely subjective. From a Vajrayana point of view, whatever work you do—whether it's as a butcher, a receptionist, or an exotic dancer—if you have the right motivation, conviction in bringing your practice to your work, and artfulness, you can be of benefit.

For my own sake, I have poked and prodded at Caitlin a few times since our initial meeting, and I have to say that I have found zero self-deception with this lady. She clearly is a kind, compassionate person who is trying to balance Buddhism and this livelihood in an effort to do the art that she loves.

Caitlin presents clients with an authentic experience. She will have a real conversation with them, as opposed to trying to flirt with them in order to lure them into giving her all their money. She will tell them about her life, her art, and even her meditation practice. She will treat them with respect, and they respect her in kind. I believe that is because she is able to manifest an authentic presence, even at a strip club.

I mention Hylke and Caitlin not just because they are both wonderful people whom I feel very lucky to have in my life, but because if they weren't so authentic I doubt I would have ever befriended them. Beyond our shared interest in meditation, there's not a whole lot we have in common. Yet I am magnetized to them, and have collaborated with them on work efforts, because I enjoy being around authentic people. Both of these individuals are real people who work to help others. They are fulfilling the aim of what Trungpa Rinpoche said the Shambhala Buddhist path is for. Their work may look different from what you and I do from nine to five, but they are genuine human beings who are not shy of manifesting who they are.

We can learn from their example and in turn become more authentically who we are. We can become truly comfortable in our skin and wield the power of our presence in a way that brings delight and relaxation to others. We can contact our basic goodness and ride the energy of that experience. When we are able to authentically do all of that, we magnetize the resources we need and provide inspiration to others.

23 / FIVE SLOGANS FOR INCREASING CONVICTION IN YOUR NATURAL STATE

Your mission, should you choose to accept it, is to drop the barrier between your work and your meditation practice. We can develop real confidence in our awakened nature, our basic goodness, and from that perspective transform whatever obstacles arise into opportunities to apply the appropriate upaya, or skillful means.

Following Tilopa's lead, you can commit yourself to skillful means, joining your work and your practice so that the two become inseparable. Part of that process is surrendering ego while cultivating virtue. These two processes together allow us to deepen our experience of our basic state and to exude an authentic presence.

There are five additional mind-training slogans of Atisha which seem particularly applicable to the Vajrayana path. Although the lojong slogans are primarily a Mahayana tool for cultivating bodhicitta, those teachings lay the foundation for the Vajrayana journey. The Vajrayana path shares in the Mahayana vision of working toward awakening in order to be of benefit to others.

Rest in the nature of alaya, the essence.

In chapter 10, we discussed the alaya consciousness—the warehouse consciousness where the imprints of our virtuous and unvirtuous activity are stored lifetime after lifetime. Here the subject is the alaya, the pure nature of that consciousness. In Traleg Rinpoche's commentary on lojong, he translates this slogan as "Rest in the natural state, the basis of all."

The nature of this alaya is wisdom mind. It is our awakened state. The Sanskrit term associated with this idea is *alaya-jnana*, or "basis of all." In this sense, we are being implored not to hang out in our warehouse but to rest in the basis of that warehouse, which is our pure, brilliant nature.

Interestingly enough, Tilopa already imparted this instruction to us. In his "Six Words of Advice," he tells us to step away from thoughts of the future, thoughts of the past, and even busying our mind or trying to control this present moment, and to just rest. That is the same advice that Atisha is offering here. Rest your mind.

When you are able to relax to this extent, you experience the essence of your being, which is wisdom mind. The renowned Tibetan Buddhist teacher Jamgön Kongtrul Rinpoche has said that the basis of everything is known as "noble buddha-nature," our awakened state. That is what we are connecting to and resting in.

It is up to you whether you want to take Atisha's advice. There are only two options, though: you can rest your mind in a chaotic, story line–based condition or in its natural, awake condition. Traleg Rinpoche recommends the latter and instructs us in how to do that: "For the natural way of resting, we simply maintain a sense of bare awareness without thinking about anything or forcing the mind into a concentrated state."[1] When we are able to be this diligent in our relaxation, our meditation practice flourishes and we live in a sane and awake manner.

In postmeditation, be a child of illusion.

When you get up after meditating, you should not just say, "Well, that was nice. I'm done with that." Instead, in your post-meditation experience, you should bring that mindfulness and compassion off the cushion and into your everyday life.

The relative teachings of the Mahayana address the principles of bodhicitta and compassion, and the absolute teachings of the Mahayana are about developing the realization that you and others—and all phenomena as well—are empty of an absolute self, or ego. This realization is the foundation for the Vajrayana path.

The second half of the slogan points to the emptiness that is the actual nature of phenomena. The instruction is to rest with our illusory experience of the phenomenal world. We don't have to take it all so seriously. We don't have to solidify our obstacles into big, insurmountable issues.

There is a traditional analogy used to explain how we misperceive reality. Imagine walking through a field late at night. All of a sudden you spot something right in your path. It's a giant snake—how horrifying! The thing is, when you shine your flashlight on it, you realize it is only a piece of rope. It is said that we misperceive reality in this exact way all the time.

We are constantly looking at our life as full of snakes, when really they are just ropes lying everywhere. In this sense, our work life is not filled with scary monsters that are out to get us; it is our flawed perception that sees things that way. Atisha is saying that we don't have to solidify phenomena in this habitual way. Instead, we can perceive whatever we encounter as sacred and magical, simply by being present to its reality. Our coworkers have basic goodness. We have basic goodness. Thus, our whole situation is sacred. When we can make this switch in view, we realize that absolutely everything is workable.

All dharma agrees at one point.

In this context, Atisha is using the term *dharma* specifically to denote the teachings of the Buddha. He is saying that the unifying aspect of everything the Buddha ever taught is the imperative to overcome our own ignorance of self and of reality. Chögyam Trungpa Rinpoche has commented on this slogan saying that in all the three yanas of Tibetan Buddhism we are asked to shed our habitual layers of ego and surrender to the way things are. That is the point where all the teachings agree.

In part 1, we studied how meditation practice on the Hinayana path cuts through habitual mind. The more you sit shamatha, the more your ego is destroyed. Because you are no longer reinforcing your constant inner gossip and story lines, they do not hold so much sway over you. You are more able to enter your workplace with a fresh perspective, as opposed to always being lost in your own head.

The Mahayana path is based in giving up our time, energy, money—really everything we have—in order to benefit others. This letting-go process destroys me-based thinking. You realize that you can offer yourself fully to your work and your world without losing anything. When you engage the bodhisattva path, you only gain.

Furthermore, you can give up your fixed views around your sense of self as well as your fixed views about other people. You can contemplate the concept of emptiness and develop conviction in your being that things are, indeed, more illusory than they appear.

Finally, on the Vajrayana path, you surrender all of your neurosis and hang-ups in order to empty yourself, making yourself a vessel to experience what is going on right now. That includes offering up your body, speech, and mind on a regular basis in order to be most fully in the moment with whatever comes up. It is that process of giving up everything, so that you can accommodate anything.

When you are able to traverse the various paths of the Buddha's teachings with this idea in mind, you are liberated from your own mental afflictions and are more available to be your most authentic self at work and at home.

Abandon any hope of fruition.

This is an interesting slogan, because so many of us begin a meditation practice with a specific goal in mind, maybe something like "I want to have less stress" or "I want to be less frustrated at work." However, as we continue on our journey, we realize that so much of how we achieve these goals is based in just being present to this very moment. Thus, we should abandon any fixed idea about what will happen in our practice or in our work life. The meaning of this slogan is that we should not be so focused on results. Worrying about results is flying in the face of Tilopa's advice: "Don't imagine" and "Let go of what may come." To fixate on what may or may not arise in the future only fuels our own game of giving in to hope and fear. If you are lost in potential outcomes for any given task at work, then you are simply distracted from the task at hand and no longer fully engaged. Instead, you can focus on what is going on right now.

Abandoning any hope of fruition means letting go of our preconceived notions of how something might work out. That something may be a particular project at work, a specific position you are seeking, or a vision for your career overall. The more we give up that set sense of what we think needs to happen, the more we can focus on making things happen here and now. In other words, don't focus on results, focus on the process. Thankfully, the more space you give yourself, the more possibilities present themselves.

Train wholeheartedly.

Our last slogan summarizes the instructions for this entire book. In all of our endeavors we should train wholeheartedly.

We need to be single-minded in bringing our full and most authentic self to every moment of our life.

Early on in the path, this means training wholeheartedly on the meditation cushion so you can be present with your breath during shamatha, cutting through your habitual patterns repeatedly. Through this process you become familiar with your own mind and are better able to discern your intention for your livelihood and life. It means training wholeheartedly in bringing mindfulness off the cushion and into your work life, so that you embody right livelihood and wield your speech as a weapon of delight. It means being present with whatever comes up in your nine to five, so you can respond in a thoughtful and considerate manner.

As you begin to acknowledge the suffering of others, your heart goes out to them and you long to be helpful. That is the basis of offering your bodhicitta. You can train wholeheartedly in cultivating this potent quality, opening your heart to people you like as well as those who get on your nerves. You can train in cultivating virtue, and avoiding activity that is unvirtuous. You can discern whom to work with and what mentors to cultivate so that you are best supported in your path. You can also train wholeheartedly in the six paramitas, those tools for offering yourself fully in the office. You can exercise diligence in cutting through fixed view, raising your gaze, and engaging in compassionate activity, no matter what.

Furthermore, you can train in leadership. You can apply yourself fully to training in the qualities of being benevolent, true, genuine, fearless, artful, and rejoicing. Through training in these Six Ways of Ruling, you learn to wield your power for the benefit of all and can create great change in the world.

Last but not least, you can train in developing confidence in your basic state, your own awake nature. It may sound obvious, but you do need to train in cultivating a sense of conviction in basic goodness. When you do, all of these other teachings emanate smoothly. Once you are in tune with your basic goodness, you can overcome any obstacles with upaya, skillful and expedient means. You are able to manifest your unique abilities in any situation. You can surrender the last vestiges of your ego and become a truly authentic person. Perhaps most important, you will be able to see the unity of your work and your practice.

This instruction to train wholeheartedly points out that we are not engaged in an easy path. In some sense, it's very easy: if you remember to live a life based in an experience of basic goodness, things flow naturally. Because we have not habituated ourselves to that point of view, we will experience upsets and doubt. That is why we need to train in all of these qualities. We need to commit to being in it for the long haul. When we have this level of commitment, we will end up living every day from the perspective of our inherent worthiness, our awake state.

When you live a life in touch with your basic goodness, you are unstoppable. There is nothing you cannot accomplish in or out of the workplace. When you work with your own mind and work to benefit others, it almost doesn't matter what career path you choose; you are already engaging your world wholeheartedly and will be successful in the most meaningful sense.

Through practicing these qualities, you can manifest as the practitioner this world needs. You can be present and engage your life as it is. You can join work and practice in a way that is true to your own noble, open heart. You can lead others with their welfare in mind and utilize these paths as a course of becoming awake. Please do it, because the world needs more leaders like you.

NOTES

CHAPTER 2. DISCOVERING OUR WORTHINESS

1. Wayne Dyer, *The Power of Intention* (Carlsbad, CA: Hay House, 2005), p. 185.

CHAPTER 4. WIELDING YOUR SPEECH LIKE
                THE HAMMER OF THOR

1. Sakyong Mipham, *Ruling Your World* (New York: Morgan Road Books, 2005), p. 32.
2. Pema Chödrön, *Living Beautifully with Uncertainty and Change* (Boston: Shambhala Publications, 2012), p. 33.
3. Henry Cloud, *Integrity* (New York: HarperBusiness, 2009), p. 59.
4. Shantideva, *The Way of the Bodhisattva*, trans. Padmakara Translation Group, rev. ed. (Boston: Shambhala Publications, 2006), ch. 5, v. 79.
5. Ibid., vv. 49–50.
6. Yamamoto Tsunetomo, *Hagakure: The Book of the Samurai*, trans. William Scott Wilson (Boston: Shambhala Publications, 2012), p. 13.

CHAPTER 5. RUSSIAN ROULETTE AND
                THE POWER OF JUST DO IT

1. Chögyam Trungpa, *Born in Tibet* (Boston: Shambhala Publications, 1966, 2000).

2. Sakyong Mipham, *The Shambhala Principle: Discovering Humanity's Hidden Treasure* (New York: Harmony Books, 2013), p. 124.
3. Shantideva, *The Way of the Bodhisattva*, ch. 5, v. 22.
4. Chögyam Trungpa, *Work, Sex, Money* (Boston: Shambhala Publications, 2011), p. 94.

CHAPTER 6. FIVE SLOGANS FOR CHANGING HOW YOU VIEW WORK

1. Traleg Kyabgon, *The Practice of Lojong* (Boston: Shambhala Publications, 2007), p. 173.
2. Chögyam Trungpa, *Collected Works*, vol. 2 (Boston: Shambhala Publications, 2010), p. 218.
3. Pema Chödrön, *Comfortable with Uncertainty* (Boston: Shambhala Publications, 2008), p. 130.

CHAPTER 7. ROM-COMS, ZOMBIES, AND BODHICITTA

1. Quoted in Gampopa, *The Jewel Ornament of Liberation,* trans. Khenpo Konchog Gyaltsen (Ithaca, NY: Snow Lion, 1998), p. 173.
2. Chögyam Trungpa, *Training the Mind and Cultivating Loving-Kindness* (Boston: Shambhala Publications, 1993), p. 28.

CHAPTER 8. MENTORS AND VIRTUE

1. Ngulchu Thogme, *The 37 Practices of a Bodhisattva*, with commentary by Khenpo Tsultrim Gyamtso Rinpoche (Kathmandu: Marpa Foundation, 2001), v. 8.
2. Tsoknyi Rinpoche, "The Meaning of Virtue and Generosity," *Huffington Post,* www.huffingtonpost.com /Tsoknyi-rinpoche/definition-virtue_b_1415747.html, accessed February 4, 2014.
3. Shantideva, *The Way of the Bodhisattva*, ch. 5, v. 55.

4. Trungpa, *Work, Sex, Money*, p. 58.
5. Tsunetomo, *Hagakure*, p. 21.

CHAPTER 9. BOMBING YOUR WORKPLACE WITH AWAKE

1. Dudjom Rinpoche, *A Torch Lighting the Way to Freedom* (Boston: Shambhala Publications, 2011).
2. Pema Chödrön, *The Places That Scare You* (Boston: Shambhala Publications, 2002), p. 95.
3. Dudjom, *Torch Lighting the Way*, p. 177.
4. Mipham, *Ruling Your World*, p. 115.

CHAPTER 10. KARMA, THE SIX REALMS, AND WHY YOU SHOULD STOP BEING A JERK

1. Sakyong Mipham, *Turning the Mind into an Ally* (New York: Penguin, 2004), p. 162.
2. Mipham, *Ruling Your World*, p. 51.

CHAPTER 11. THREE STEPS FOR CREATING SOCIAL CHANGE THROUGH INNER CHANGE

1. Career Advisory Board, *The Future of Millennial Careers*, http://careeradvisoryboard.org/research/the-future -of-millennial-careers-research.
2. Dev Patnaik, "Innovation Starts with Empathy," http:// designmind.frogdesign.com/articles/the -substance-of-things-not-seen/innovation-starts-with -empathy.html.
3. Tsunetomo, *Hagakure*, p. 45.

CHAPTER 12. FIVE SLOGANS FOR EMPATHY AND COMPASSION

1. Trungpa, *Collected Works*, vol. 2, p. 179.
2. Ibid., p. 161.

3. Bronnie Ware, *The Top Five Regrets of the Dying* (Carlsbad, CA: Hay House, 2012).

CHAPTER 13. BENEVOLENCE, OR BASHING AGGRESSION WITH THE VELVET HAMMER

1. Marcus Buckingham and Curt Coffman, *First, Break All the Rules* (New York: Simon & Schuster, 1999).
2. From a talk by Sakyong Mipham, given at "Being Brave: A Shambhala Retreat," held at Karmê Chöling, Vermont, May 2012.

CHAPTER 14. TRUE, OR HOW TO BE STEADY AS A MOUNTAIN

1. Trungpa, *Collected Works*, vol. 8, p. 66.
2. Olivia Fox Cabane, "How to Reverse Your Hardwiring for Distraction," www.fastcompany.com/1830292/how-reverse-your-hard-wiring-distraction.

CHAPTER 15. GENUINE, OR POINTING TO THE STARS

1. Trungpa, *Collected Works*, vol. 2, p. 144.
2. Will Durant, *The Story of Philosophy* (Simon & Schuster/Pocket Books, 1926, 1991).

CHAPTER 17. ARTFULNESS, OR ARRANGING YOUR KINGDOM

1. Tina Fey, *Bossypants* (New York: Back Bay Books, 2012).
2. Tsunetomo, *Hagakure*, p. 36.

CHAPTER 20. IT'S HARD OUT HERE FOR A PIMP

1. Cited in Tulku Thondup, "The Power of Positive Karma," www.shambhalasun.com/index.php?option=com_content&task=view&id=2914&Itemid=0.
2. Judith Simmer-Brown, *Dakini's Warm Breath* (Boston: Shambhala Publications, 2002).

3. Tilopa, "Six Words of Advice," trans. Ken McLeod, www.unfetteredmind.org/six-words-of-advice.

CHAPTER 21. LET GO OF MY EGO

1. Trungpa, *Collected Works*, vol. 3, p. 23.

CHAPTER 22. STRIPPERS, LIFE COACHES, AND CULTIVATING AN AUTHENTIC PRESENCE

1. Trungpa, *Collected Works*, vol. 8, p. 177.

CHAPTER 23. FIVE SLOGANS FOR INCREASING CONVICTION IN YOUR NATURAL STATE

1. Kyabgon, *Practice of Lojong*, p. 57.

RESOURCES

FURTHER READING

Buckingham, Marcus, and Curt Coffman. *First, Break All the Rules: What the World's Greatest Managers Do Differently.* New York: Simon & Schuster, 1999. An insightful read that breaks the mold of a traditional business book.

Carroll, Michael. *Awake at Work: 35 Practical Buddhist Principles for Discovering Clarity and Balance in the Midst of Work's Chaos.* Boston: Shambhala Publications, 2004. The author has spent decades applying meditation principles to the workplace environment.

———. *Fearless at Work: Timeless Teachings for Awakening Confidence, Resilience, and Creativity in the Face of Life's Demands.* Boston: Shambhala Publications, 2012. An excellent exploration of fearlessness.

Chödrön, Pema. *Comfortable with Uncertainty: 108 Teachings on Cultivating Fearlessness and Compassion.* Boston: Shambhala Publications, 2002. A compilation of teachings from Pema Chödrön, each chapter short enough to read in a few minutes before bed.

Fincher, Susanne F. *Creating Mandalas.* Boston: Shambhala Publications, 1991. For more information on mandalas.

Mipham, Sakyong. *Ruling Your World: Ancient Strategies for Modern Life.* New York: Morgan Road Books, 2005. A great book overall, but a terrific exploration of the Six Ways of Ruling.

———. *The Shambhala Principle: Discovering Humanity's Hidden Treasure.* New York: Harmony Books, 2013. A practical manifesto on how basic goodness can create a better tomorrow.

———. *Turning the Mind into an Ally.* New York: Riverhead Books, 2003. My recommended go-to read for the technique of meditation.

Nichtern, Ethan. *One City: A Declaration of Interdependence.* Somerville, Mass.: Wisdom Publications, 2007. Great further reading on the topic of karma.

Shantideva. *The Way of the Bodhisattva.* Translated by Padmakara Translation Group. Revised edition. Boston: Shambhala Publications, 2006. A pivotal text on the Mahayana path.

Simmer-Brown, Judith. *Dakini's Warm Breath: The Feminine Principle in Tibetan Buddhism.* Boston: Shambhala Publications, 2001. A wonderful, full explanation of the role of the dakini in Tibetan Buddhism.

Thogme, Ngulchu. *The 37 Practices of a Bodhisattva.* Commentary by Khenpo Tsultrim Gyamtso Rinpoche. Kathmandu: Marpa Foundation, 2001. Each practice is worth spending at least a day contemplating.

Trungpa, Chögyam. *Shambhala: The Sacred Path of the Warrior.* Boston: Shambhala Publications, 1984. A foundational text on Shambhala Buddhism.

———. *Work, Sex, Money: Real Life on the Path of Mindfulness.* Boston: Shambhala Publications, 2011. A beautiful exposition of the intersection of work and meditation.

WEB SITES

www.shambhala.org. Teachings and resources for supporting your meditation practice, including a list of Shambhala Centers that you can visit for in-person teachings.

www.lodrorinzler.com. My personal Web site with written, audio, and video teachings, and the best way to get in touch with me directly.

www.instituteforcompassionateleadership.org. The Web site for the Institute for Compassionate Leadership, my nonprofit training program based partly in the principles explained in this book.

www.samadhicushions.com. A great source for meditation cushions, malas, and other supplies.

www.reciprocityfoundation.org. Profits from meditation cushions go toward supporting homeless youth in New York City.

LOJONG

If you found the mind-training teachings helpful, you can purchase lojong cards online or from a meditation shop and set them up in your home or on your desk. Alternatively, you can find the slogans in a book or on the Web and make your own cards. If you would like to contemplate the lojong slogans in depth, I recommend you take one a day and contemplate what it means to you.

For example, you can flip to a new card, rest your mind for a moment, and then read the slogan one to three times, aloud or to yourself. See what meaning comes up in response to the words on the card. See how the teaching may be relevant to your life. When your mind wanders off, bring it back to the phrase on the card, just like you bring your attention back to your breath in shamatha meditation. After a few minutes, return to your regular meditation practice, resting your mind on the breath.

When you conclude your contemplation, you can see what meaning remains with you. See if the lojong slogan can be applied to your work or home life and how it plays out in the course of that day. If you forget or you struggle with a particular slogan, there is always a new one the next day.